STUDY GUIDE FOR USE WITH

Fundamental Accounting Principles

VOLUME 1

TENTH CANADIAN EDITION

KERMIT D. LARSON
University of Texas at Austin, Emeritus

TILLY JENSEN
Northern Alberta Institute of Technology

RAY CARROLL
Dalhousie University

Prepared by
SUZANNE COOMBS
Kwantlen University College

 **McGraw-Hill Ryerson**

Toronto Montréal Boston Burr Ridge, IL Dubuque, IA Madison, WI New York San Francisco
St. Louis Bangkok Bogotá Caracas Kuala Lumpur Lisbon London Madrid
Mexico City Milan New Delhi Santiago Seoul Singapore Sydney Taipei

McGraw-Hill
Ryerson Limited

A Subsidiary of The McGraw-Hill Companies

Study Guide, Volume 1, Chapters 1-11
for use with
FUNDAMENTAL ACCOUNTING PRINCIPLES, Tenth Canadian Edition

ISBN: 0-07-088986-4

4 5 6 7 8 9 10 MP 0 9 8 7 6 5 4 3

Printed and bound in Canada

Care has been taken to trace ownership of copyright material contained in this text; however, the publisher will welcome any information that enables them to rectify any reference or credit for subsequent editions.

Vice President and Editorial Director: Pat Ferrier
Senior Sponsoring Editor: Nicole Lukach
Developmental Editor: Katherine Goodes
Supervising Editor: Carrie Withers
Senior Marketing Manager: Jeff MacLean
Production Coordinator: Madeleine Harrington
Printer: Maracle Press, Ltd.

Contents

Learning Objective 5:

Identify users and uses of accounting.

Summary

There are both internal and external users of accounting. Some users and uses of accounting include: (a) management for control, monitoring and planning; (b) lenders for making decisions regarding loan applications; (c) shareholders for making investment decisions; (d) directors for overseeing management; and (e) employees for judging employment opportunities.

Learning Objective 6:

Explain why ethics and social responsibility are crucial to accounting.

Summary

The goal of accounting is to provide useful information for decision making. For information to be useful it must be trusted. This demands ethics and socially responsible behaviour in accounting. Without these, accounting information loses its reliability.

Learning Objective 7:

Identify opportunities in accounting and related fields.

Summary

Opportunities in accounting and related fields are numerous. They include traditional ones like financial, managerial and tax accounting. They also include accounting related fields such as lending, consulting, managing and planning.

Learning Objective 8:

Explain e-business and identify other technology applications useful to accounting.

Summary

E-business, also known as e-commerce, is the operation of a business online. Many businesses conduct sales transactions on the Internet while others use it for marketing purposes. Difficulties created because of online transactions include unlawful tampering of systems and the inability of tax collection agencies, like the CCRA, to track sales. Accounting software applications have made the recording, processing, and storing of accounting information more efficient.

Chapter Outline

I.   **Accounting in the changing global economy**—technology allows instant access to services, data, news and information to aid business operations

    A. Power of Accounting

        The power of accounting is in opening our eyes to new and exciting opportunities. *Accounting* is an information system that identifies, measures, records and communicates relevant, reliable and comparable information about an organization's economic activities. to help people make better decisions.

    B. Focus of Accounting

        The primary objective of accounting is to provide useful information for decision-making. Accounting information results from activities such as identifying, measuring, recording, reporting and analyzing economic events and transactions. Accounting also involves designing information systems to provide useful reports to monitor and control an organization's activities. Accounting involves recordkeeping, or bookkeeping, but is much more.

    C. Role of Accounting in Business

        1. Business Profit

            Profit (net income, or earnings) is the amount a business earns after subtracting all *expenses* necessary to earn *revenues* (revenues – expenses = profit). *Revenues (sales)* are the amounts earned from selling products and services. *Expenses* are the costs incurred to generate (or produce) revenues. A *net loss* arises when expenses are more than revenues.

II. **Forms of Organization**

  A. Business Organization

    The *business entity principle* (GAAP) states that each economic entity or business of the owner must keep accounting records and reports separate from the owner and any other economic entity of the owner. There are three forms of business organization and each form has implications to legal entity, limited liability, unlimited life, business taxation, and number of owners. The three forms are:

    1. *Sole Proprietorship* is a business owned by one person who is subject to unlimited liability. Because tax authorities do not separate a proprietorship from its owner, the profits of the business are reported and taxed on the owner's personal income tax return.

    2. *Partnership* is a business owned by two or more persons, called partners, who are subject to unlimited liability. Because the business is not legally separate from its owners, each partner's share of profits is reported and taxed on that partner's tax return.

    3. *Corporation* is a business that is a separate legal entity whose owners are called shareholders. These owners have limited liability. The entity is responsible for a business income tax and the owners are responsible for personal income tax on profits that are distributed to them in the form of dividends.

  B. Nonbusiness organizations plan and operate for goals other than profit. They do not have an identifiable owner.

III.   Users and Uses of Accounting Information

    A. External information users are those not directly involved in running the organization.

        1. External reports called financial statements help users analyze an organization's activities. These reports must follow rules referred to as GAAP.

        2. External Users—lenders, shareholders, external auditors, employees, regulators, and others.

        3. Financial accounting is aimed at serving external users.

    B. Internal information users are directly involved in managing and operating an organization.

        1. Managerial accounting is aimed at serving the decision-making needs of internal users. Special purpose reports are customized to meet the information needs of internal users.

        2. Internal operating functions rely on accounting information to ensure the smooth operation of each function.

        3. Internal controls are procedures set up to protect assets, ensure reliable accounting reports, promote efficiency, and ensure company policies are followed.

IV.   Ethics and Social Responsibility

    A. Understanding Ethics—Ethics are beliefs that separate right from wrong.

        1. Ethical behaviour is important to the accounting profession and to those who use accounting information.

        2. A lack of ethics makes it more difficult for people to trust one another. Ethical behaviour is necessary in accounting if the information it provides is to be trusted.

        3. Accountants have ethical obligations. They are expected to maintain a high level of professional competence, treat sensitive information confidential, exercise personal integrity, and be objective in matters of financial disclosure.

    B. Organizational Ethics—are likely learned through management example and leadership.

    C. Accounting Ethics—are crucial.

        1. Misleading information can lead to incorrect decisions, seriously harming workers, customers and suppliers.

        2. Codes of ethics for accountants are set up and enforced by the provincial offices of all of the professional accounting bodies.

    D. Social Responsibility—is a concern for the impact of our actions on society as a whole. Organizations are concerned with their social responsibility.

V.   **Accounting Opportunities**

   A. There are four broad fields within accounting

   1. *Financial Accounting* serves the needs of external users by providing financial statements. An audit is an independent review and test of an organization's accounting systems and record. External auditors perform the audit function.

   2. *Managerial Accounting* serves the needs of internal users by providing special purpose reports in areas such as:

   a. General Accounting

   b. Cost Accounting

   c. Budgeting

   d. Internal Auditing

   e. Management Consulting

   3. *Tax Accounting* involves tax consultation, planning, and the preparation of tax returns.

   4. *Accounting-Related* opportunities include lending, consulting, managing, planning and other roles.

   B. Professional Certification—In Canada, several accounting organizations provide the education and training required to obtain professional certification. The three professional accounting designations are:

   1. Chartered Accountant (CA)

   2. Certified General Accountant (CGA)

   3. Certified Management Accountant (CMA)

VI.   **Appendix 1—Accounting and Technology**

   A. E-Business (e-commerce) — is when a business goes online.

   B. Implications of e-business for accounting

   1. The accounting information system must be able to record transactions that occur online.

   2. The CCRA, the Canadian taxing authority, must ensure that it is collection income from all e-commerce business.

   3. Unauthorized persons may tamper with a computer system. Steps need to be taken to ensure that once an accounting information systems based on new technologies is in place, it is protected from potential compromise.

Problem I

Many of the important ideas and concepts discussed in Chapter 1 are reflected in the following list of key terms. Test your understanding of these terms by matching the appropriate definitions with the terms. Record the number identifying the most appropriate definition in the blank space next to each term.

14	Accounting		Internal auditors
	Audit	28	Internal controls
27	Bookkeeping	8	Internal users
	Budgeting	36	Limited liability
47	Business	18	Limited liabilities partnership
	Business entity principle	34	Limited partnership
4	CA		Management consulting
25	CCRA	10	Managerial accounting
20	CGA	46	Net income
13	CMA	26	Net loss
1	Common share	3	Partnership
	Controller	44	Private accountants
32	Corporation	21	Profit
	Cost accounting	12	Public accountants
24	Earnings	37	Recordkeeping
7	E-business	40	Revenues
42	Expenses	22	Sales
	External auditors	15	Shareholders
31	External users	43	Shares
33	Ethics	29	Single proprietorship
45	Financial accounting	16	Social responsibility
9	GAAP	25	Tax accounting
17	General accounting		Unlimited liability
23	Government accountants		

1. The name for a corporation's shares when only one class of share capital is issued.

2. Employees within organizations who assess whether managers are following established operating procedures and evaluate the efficiency of operating procedures.

3. A business that is owned by two or more people that is not organized as a corporation.

4. When the debts of a sole proprietorship or partnership are greater than its resources, the owner(s) is financially responsible.

5. Every business is accounted for separately from its owner's personal activities.

6. A managerial accounting activity designed to help managers identify, measure and control operating costs.

7. Conducting business online; commonly sales transactions and/or marketing.

8. Persons using accounting information who are directly involved in managing and operating an organization; examples include managers and officers.

9. Generally accepted accounting principles are the rules that indicate acceptable accounting practise.

10. The area of accounting aimed at serving the decision-making needs of internal users.

---

11. The field of accounting that includes preparing tax returns and planning future transactions to minimize the amount of tax; involves private, public, and governmental accountants.

12. Accountants who provide their services to many different clients.

13. Certified Management Accountant; an accountant who has met the examination, education and experience requirements of the Society of Management Accountants for an individual professionally competent in accounting

14. An information system that identifies, measures, records and communicates relevant, reliable, and comparable information about an organization's economic activities.

15. The owners of a corporation.

16. Involves considering the impact and being accountable for the effects that actions might have on society.

17. The task of recording transactions, processing data, and preparing reports for managers; includes preparing financial statements for disclosure to external users.

18. Restricts partners' liabilities to their own acts and the acts of individuals under their control.

19. A check of an organization's accounting systems and records.

20. Examine and provide assurance that financial statements are prepared according to generally accepted accounting principles (GAAP).

21. The amount a business earns after subtracting all expenses incurred to generate revenues; also called net income or earnings.

22. The amounts earned from selling products or services; also called revenues.

23. Work for local, provincial and federal government agencies.

24. The amount a business earns after subtracting all expenses necessary to create revenues; also called net income or profit.

25. Canada Customs and Revenue Agency; the federal government agency responsible for the collection of tax and enforcement of tax laws.

26. Arises when total expenses are more than revenues (sales).

27. The part of accounting that involves recording economic transactions and events, either electronically or manually; also called record keeping.

28. Procedures set up to protect assets, ensure reliable accounting reports, promote efficiency, and encourage adherence to company policies.

29. A business owned by one individual that is not organized as a corporation; also called a sole proprietorship.

30. The chief accounting officer of an organization.

31. Persons using accounting information who are not directly involved in the running of the organization; examples include shareholders, customers, regulators, and suppliers.

32. A business that is a separate legal entity under provincial or federal laws with owners that are called shareholders.

Fundamental Accounting Principles, 10th Canadian Edition

33. Beliefs that separate right from wrong.

34. Includes both general partner(s) with unlimited liability and a limited partner(s) with liability restricted to the amount invested.

35. Certified General Accountant; an accountant who has met the examination, education and experience requirements of the Certified General Accountants' Association for an individual professionally competent in accounting.

36. The owner's liability is limited to their investment in the business..

37. The recording of financial transactions and events, either manually or electronically; also called bookkeeping.

38. The process of developing formal plans for future activities, which often serve as a basis for evaluating actual performance.

39. Activity in which suggestions are offered for improving a company's procedures; the suggestions may concern new accounting and internal control systems, new computer systems, budgeting, and employee benefit plans.

40. The amounts earned from selling products or services; also called sales.

41. Chartered Accountant; an accountant who has met the examination, education and experience requirements of the Institute of Chartered Accountants for an individual professionally competent in accounting.

42. The costs incurred to earn revenues (or sales).

43. A unit of ownership in a corporation.

44. Accountants who work for a single employer other than the government or a public accounting firm.

45. The area of accounting aimed at serving external users.

46. The amount a business earns after subtracting all expenses incurred to general revenues; also called profit or earnings.

47. One of more individuals selling products or services for profit.

Solutions for Chapter 1

Problem I

Accounting	14	Government accountants	23
Audit	19	Internal auditors	2
Bookkeeping	27	Internal controls	28
Budgeting	38	Internal users	8
Business	47	Limited liability	36
Business entity principle	5	Limited liability partnership	18
CA	41	Limited partnership	34
CCRA	25	Management consulting	39
CGA	35	Managerial accounting	10
CMA	13	Net income	46
Common share	1	Net loss	26
Controller	30	Partnership	3
Corporation	32	Private accountants	44
Cost accounting	6	Profit	21
Earnings	24	Public accountants	12
E-business	7	Recordkeeping	37
Expenses	42	Revenues	40
External auditors	20	Sales	22
External users	31	Shareholders	15
Ethics	33	Shares	43
Financial accounting	45	Single proprietorship	29
GAAP	9	Social responsibility	16
General accounting	17	Tax accounting	11
		Unlimited liability	4

Learning Objective 1:

Identify and explain the content and reporting aims of financial statements.

Summary

The major financial statements are: income statement, balance sheet, statement of changes in owner's equity, and statement of cash flows. An income statement shows a company's profitability including revenues, expenses and net income (loss). A balance sheet reports on a company's financial position including assets, liabilities and owner's equity. A statement of owner's equity explains how owner's equity changes from the beginning to the end of a period, and the statement of cash flows identifies all cash inflows and outflows for the period.

Learning Objective 2:

Identify differences in financial statements across forms of business organization.

Summary

One important difference is in the equity section of the balance sheet. A proprietorship's and partnership's balance sheet lists the equity balance beside the owner's name. Names of a corporation's shareholders are not listed in a balance sheet. Another difference is with the term used to describe distributions by a business to its owners. When an owner of a proprietorship or a partnership takes cash or other assets from a company, the distributions are called withdrawals. When owners of a corporation receive cash or other assets from a company, the distributions are called dividends. Recording payments to managers when managers are also owners is another difference. When the owner of a proprietorship or partnership is its manager, no salary expense is reported. But since a corporation is a separate legal entity, salaries paid to its employees, including managers who are also shareholders, are always reported as expenses on its income statement.

Learning Objective 3:

Identify, explain and apply accounting principles.

Summary

Accounting principles aid in producing relevant, reliable, consistent, and comparable information. The general principles described in this chapter include: business entity, objectivity, cost, going-concern, monetary unit, and revenue recognition. We will discuss others in later chapters. The business entity principle means that a business is accounted for separately from its owner. The objectivity principle means information is supported by independent, objective evidence. The cost principle means financial statements are based on actual costs incurred in business transactions. He going-concern principle means financial statements reflect an assumption that the business continues operating. The monetary unit principle assumes transactions and events can be captured in money terms and that the monetary unit is stable over time. The revenue recognition principle means revenue is recognized when earned, that assets received from selling products and services do not have to be in cash, and that revenue recognized is measured by cash received plus the cash equivalent (market) value of other assets received.

Learning Objective 4:

Explain and interpret the accounting equation.

Summary

Investing activities are funded by an organization's financing activities. An organization's assets (investments) must equal its financing (from liabilities and from equity). This basic relation gives us the accounting equation: Assets = Liabilities + Owner's Equity.

Learning Objective 5:

Analyze business transactions using the accounting equation.

Summary

A transaction is an exchange of economic consideration between two parties. Examples of economic considerations include products, services, money and rights to collect money. Because two different parties exchange assets and liabilities, transactions affect the components of the accounting equation. Business transactions always have at least two effects on the components of the accounting equation. The equation is always in balance when business transactions are properly recorded.

Learning Objective 6:

Prepare financial statements from business transactions.

Summary

Using the accounting equation, business transactions can be summarized and organized so we can readily prepare the financial statements. The balance sheet uses the ending balances in the accounting equation at a point in time. The statement of owner's equity and the income statement use data from the owner's equity account for the period.

Learning Objective 7: (Appendix 2A)

Describe the process by which generally accepted accounting principles are established.

Summary

Specific accounting principles for financial accounting are established in Canada by the Accounting Standards Board (AcSB), with input from various contributing bodies. Auditing standards are established by the Auditing Standards Board (ASB). The International Accounting Standards Committee (IASC) identifies preferred practices and encourages their adoption throughout the world.

Chapter Outline

Notes

I. **Communicating with Financial Statements**
Organizations report their accounting information to internal and external users in the form of financial statements. Statements reveal an organization's financial health and performance.

A. Previewing Financial Statements
There are four major financial statements: income statement, balance sheet, statement of owner's equity, and statement of cash flows. Statements are linked in time in that a balance sheet reports on an organization's financial position at a *point in time*, whereas the income statement, statement of owner's equity, and statement of cash flows report on transactions over a *period of time,* resulting in a new balance sheet at the end of the period. A one-year reporting, known as the accounting or fiscal year, is common.

1. *The income statement* reports revenues earned less expenses incurred by a business over a period of time.

   a. *Revenues*—inflows of assets in exchange for products and services provided to customers as part of the business's primary operations.

   b. *Expenses*—outflows or the using up of assets from providing products and service to customers.

   c. Net income (profit) — revenues exceed expenses; or net loss— expenses exceed revenues.

2. *The statement of owner's equity* reports on changes in equity over the reporting period. The statement starts with beginning equity and adjust it for events that increase it or decrease it.

   a. Increases occur with investments by the owner and/or net income.

   b. Decreases occur with withdrawals by the owner and/or a net loss.

3. *The balance sheet, or statement of financial position,* reports the financial position of the business at a point in time, usually at the end of a month or year, by listing the assets, liabilities and equity in a format that proves the accounting equation.

   a. *Assets*—properties or economic resources owned by the business. Common characteristic is the ability to provide future benefits to the company.

   b. *Liabilities*—obligations of a business, or claims of others against assets. A common characteristic is the capacity to reduce future assets or to require future services or products.

   c. *Equity*—is the owner's claim to the assets or the residual interest in the assets of a business after deducting liabilities; also called *net assets.*

4. *The statement of cash flows* describes the sources and uses of cash for a reporting period. The cash flows are classified as being caused by operating, investing, and financing activities. The statement also reports the beginning, ending and change in cash.

B. Financial Statements and Forms of Organizations

1. The equity section on the balance sheet is called owner's equity for a sole proprietorship, partners' equity for a partnership, and shareholders' equity for a corporation.

2. Distributions to owners are called withdrawals in a sole proprietorship, withdrawals in a partnership, and Dividends in a corporation.

3. When managers are also owners, their salaries are not an expense in a sole proprietorship, not an expense in a partnership, and an expense in a corporation.

Fundamental Accounting Principles, 10ᵗʰ Canadian Edition

Chapter Outline

Notes

II. **Generally Accepted Accounting Principles (GAAP)**

A. Setting Accounting Principles

The responsibility for setting accounting principles is determined by individuals and groups as discussed in Appendix 2A.

B. Fundamental Principles of Accounting

General principles, stemming from long-used accounting practices, are the basic assumptions, concepts and guidelines for preparing financial statements. Specific principles are detailed rules used in reporting on business transactions and events and arise more often from the rulings of authoritative groups.

1. *Business entity principle (Economic entity principle)*—each business or economic entity of the owner must keep accounting records and reports separate from the owner and any other economic entity of the owner.

2. *Objectivity principle*—financial statement information must be supported by independent, unbiased, and verifiable evidence.

3. *Cost principle*—all transactions are recorded based on the actual cash amount received or paid. The cash or cash-equivalent amount of the exchange is recorded.

4. *Going-concern principle (Continuing-concern principle)*—financial statements assume that the statements reflect a business that is going to continue its operations instead of being closed or sold.

5. *Monetary unit principle (Stable-dollar principle)*—transactions are expressed using units of money as the common denominator. It is assumed that the monetary unit is stable therefore when a transaction is originally recorded it is not later adjusted for changes in currency value or inflation.

6. *Revenue recognition principle (Realization principle)*—revenue is recorded at the time it is earned regardless of whether cash or another asset has been exchanged. The amount of revenue to be recorded is measured by the cash plus the cash equivalent market value of any other assets received.

Note: General principles described in later chapters include the time period, matching, materiality, full-disclosure, consistency, and conservatism principles.

III. Transactions and the Accounting Equation

A. The accounting equation (or balance sheet equation) describes the relationship between a company's assets, liabilities, and equity. It is expressed as: Assets = Liabilities + Owner's Equity.

B. Transaction Analysis— A business transaction is an exchange of economic consideration between two parties that causes a change in the accounting equation. Every transaction leaves the equation in balance.

1. Investment by owner =
+Asset (Cash) = + Owner's Equity (Owner's Name, Capital)
Increase on both sides of equation keeps equation in balance.

2. Purchased supplies for cash =
+Asset (Supplies) = −Asset (Cash)
Increase and decrease on one side of the equation keeps the equation in balance.

3. Purchase furniture for cash =
+ Asset (Furniture) = − Asset (Cash)
Increase and decrease on one side of the equation keeps the equation in balance.

4. Purchase furniture and supplies on credit =
+Asset (Supplies) +Asset (Furniture) = + Liability (Accounts Payable)
Increases on both sides of equation keeps equation in balance.

5. Services rendered cash =
+ Asset (Cash) = + Owner's Equity (Owner's Name, Capital)
Reason: revenue earned
Increase on both sides of equation keeps equation in balance.

6. & 7. Payment of expenses in cash =
− Asset (Cash) = − Owner's Equity (Owner's Name, Capital)
Reason: expenses (salaries, rent, etc.) incurred
Decrease on both sides of equation keeps equation in balance.

8. Services and rental revenues rendered for credit =
+ Asset (Accounts Receivable) = + Owner's Equity (Owner's Name, Capital)
Reason: revenue earned
Increase on both sides of equation keeps equation in balance.

    9. Receipt of cash on account =
+ Asset (Cash) = – Asset (Accounts Receivable)
Increase and decrease on one side of the equation keeps equation in balance.

    10. Payment of an accounts payable =
– Asset (Cash) = – Liability (Accounts Payable)
Decrease on both sides of equation keeps equation in balance.

    11. Withdrawal of cash by owner =
– Asset (Cash) = – OE (Owner's Name, Capital)
Decrease on both sides of equation keeps equation in balance.

IV. Financial Statements

Financial statements were described at the beginning of this chapter. This section shows how financial statements are prepared from business transactions.

    A. Income Statement—individual revenues and expenses are listed in the owner's equity column. Total revenues minus total expenses equals net income or loss. The statement explains how owner's equity changes during a period due to earnings activities.

    B. Statement Owner's Equity—the beginning owner's equity is taken from the owner's equity column and any investments of owner shown in this column are added. The net income from the income statement is added (or the net loss is subtracted) and the owner's withdrawals, found in the owner's equity column, are subtracted to arrive at the ending capital. The statement explains changes in equity over a period of time.

    C. Balance Sheet—the ending balance of each asset is listed and the total of this listing equals total assets. The ending balance of each liability is listed and the total equals total liabilities. The ending capital, taken from the statement of owner's equity, is listed and added to total liabilities to get total liabilities and owner's equity. This total must agree with total assets to prove the accounting equation. This statement describes a business's financial position at a point in time.

V. Developing Accounting Standards—(Appendix 2A)

    A. Generally Accepted Accounting Principles (GAAP)—are identified in response to the needs of users and other affected by accounting, and are developed primarily by the Accounting Standards Board (AcSB). Audits are performed in accordance with Generally Accepted Auditing Standards (GAAS) which are developed by the Auditing Standards Board (ASB). Finalized recommendations from these bodies are published as part of the CICA Handbook, having the force of law under the Canada Business Corporations Act.

    B. International Accounting Standards—are addressed by the International Accounting Standards Committee (IASC), which identifies preferred accounting practices and then encourages their worldwide acceptance.

BASIC ACCOUNTING EQUATION

ASSETS = LIABILITIES + OWNER'S EQUITY

Warning: No matter what happens always keep this scale in balance

TRANSACTION ANALYSIS RULES

1) Every transaction affects at least two items.

2) Every transaction must result in a balanced equation.

TRANSACTION ANALYSIS POSSIBILITIES:

A	=	L + OE
(1) +	And	+
Or (2) -	And	-
Or (3) + and -	And	No change
Or (4) No change	And	+ and -

Problem I

The following statements are either true or false. Place a (T) in the parentheses before each true statement and an (F) before each false statement.

1. (F) Equipment appraised at $12,000 and worth that much to its purchaser should be recorded at its worth ($12,000), even though it was purchased on sale for $10,000.

2. (T) The owner of a business must keep accounting records for the business separate from personal records.

3. (F) The statement of financial position shows a company's revenues, expenses, and net income or loss.

4. (P) Net income + Owner investments – Owner withdrawals = The increase in assets during the year.

5. (T) Revenue is recorded at the time it is earned regardless of whether cash or another asset has been exchanged.

Problem II

You are given several words, phrases, or numbers to choose from in completing each of the following statements or in answering the following questions. In each case select the one that best completes the statement, or answers the question, and place its letter in the answer space provided.

_____b_____ 1. Financial statement information about Boom Company is as follows:

December 31, 2001:

      Assets $27,000

      Liabilities 20,000

December 31, 2002:

      Assets 30,000

      Liabilities.. 13,600

During 2002:

      Net income 14,000

      Owner investments .... ?

      Owner withdrawals.. 16,000

The amount of owner investments during 2002 is:

a. $2,000.

b. $11,400.

c. $14,000.

d. $0.

e. Some other amount.

_____ 2. The board that currently has the primary authority to identify generally accepted accounting principles is the:

    a.   OSC.

    b.   AcSB.

    c.   FEI

    d.   ASB

    e.   CICA

_d_____ 3. The objectivity principle:

    a.   Provides guidance on when revenue should be reflected on the income statement; revenue should be recognized at the time it is earned; allows the inflow of assets associated with revenue may be in a form other than cash, and the amount of revenue should be measured as the cash plus the cash equivalent value of any noncash assets received from customers in exchange for goods or services.

    b.   Requires financial statements to reflect the assumption that the business will continue operating instead of being closed or sold, unless evidence shows that it will not continue.

    c.   Requires that every business be accounted for separately from its owner or owners.

    d.   Requires that financial statement information be supported by unbiased evidence, rather than someone's opinion.

    e.   Requires that financial statements be based on actual costs incurred in business transactions; where cost is cash or cash-equivalent amount given in exchange.

_b_____ 4. Obligations of a business or organization or claims against assets, are called:

    a. Assets.

    b. Liabilities

    c. Expenses.

    d. Revenues.

    e. Owner's equity.

_e_____ 5. Of the four major financial statements , three of the statement report on transactions over a period of time, and one statement reports on an organization's financial position at a point in time. The statement reporting on the financial position at a point in time is the:

    a. Income statement.

    b. Statement of owner's equity.

    c. Statement of cash flows.

    d. Statement of assets.

    e. Balance sheet.

Problem III

Many of the important ideas and concepts discussed in Chapter 2 are reflected in the following list of key terms. Test your understanding of these terms by matching the appropriate definitions with the terms. Record the number identifying the most appropriate definition in the blank space next to each term.

_____ Accounting equation	_____ GAAP
_____ Accounts payable	_____ GAAS
_____ Accounts receivable	_____ Going-concern principle
_____ AcSB	_____ IASC
_____ ASB	_____ Income statement
_____ Assets	_____ Liabilities
_____ Balance sheet	_____ Monetary unit principle
_____ Balance sheet equation	_____ Natural business year
_____ Business entity principle	_____ Net assets
_____ Business transaction	_____ Net income
_____ Calendar year	_____ Net loss
_____ CICA Handbook	_____ Notes payable
_____ Continuing-concern principle	_____ Objectivity principle
_____ Cost principle	_____ Owner investments
_____ Creditors	_____ Revenue recognition principle
_____ Debtors	_____ Revenues
_____ Dividends	_____ Statement of cash flow
_____ Equity	_____ Statement of owner's equity
_____ Expenses	_____ Statement of financial position
_____ Financial statements	_____ Withdrawal
_____ Fiscal year	

1. The principle that requires every business to be accounted for separately from its owner or owners; based on the goal of providing relevant information about each business to users.

2. Accounting Standards Board: The authoritative committee that identifies generally accepted accounting standards.

3. A 12-month period that ends when a company's sales activities are at their lowest point.

4. A financial statement that describes the sources and uses of cash for a reporting period, i.e., where a company's cash came from (receipts) and where it went during the period (payments); the cash flows are arranged by an organization's major activities: operating, investing, and financing activities.

5. The rule that requires financial statements to reflect the assumption that the business will continue operating instead of being closed or sold, unless evidence shows that it will not continue; also called *continuing-concern principle*.

6. The distribution of cash or other assets from a proprietorship or partnership to its owner or owners.

7. Individuals or organizations entitled to receive payments from a company.

8. A description of the relationship between a company's asset, liabilities, and equity; expressed as Assets = Liabilities + Owner's Equity; also called the *balance sheet equation.*.

9. The publications of the CICA that establishes generally accepted accounting principles in Canada.

10. The obligations of a business; claims by others that will reduce the future assets of a business or require future services or products.

Fundamental Accounting Principles, 10th Canadian Edition

11. The accounting guideline that requires financial statement information to be supported by independent, unbiased evidence rather than someone" opinion; objectivity adds to the reliability, verifiability, and usefulness of accounting information.

12. Another name for the balance sheet.

13. Another name for equity.

14. A liability expressed by a written promise to make a future payment at a specific time.

15. An accounting year that begins January 1 and ends December 31.

16. The most important products of accounting; include the balance sheet, income statement, statement of owner's equity, and the statement of cash flows.

17. Another name for the accounting equation.

18. The transfer of an owner's personal assets to their business.

19. The financial statement that shows whether the business earned a profit by subtracting expenses from revenues; it lists the types and amounts of revenues earned and expenses incurred by a business over a period of time.

20. Reports the changes in equity over the reporting period; beginning equity is adjusted for increases such as owner investment or net income and for decreases such as owner withdrawals or a net loss.

21. A financial statement that reports the financial position of a business at a point in time; lists the types and dollar amounts of assets, liabilities, and equity as of a specific date; also called the *statement of financial position*.

22. A one-year reporting period.

23. An economic event that changes the financial position of an organization; often takes the form of an exchange of economic consideration (such as goods, services, money, or rights to collect money) between two parties.

24. The expression of transactions and events in money units; examples include units such as the dollar, peso, and pound sterling..

25. Inflows of assets received in exchange for goods or services provided to customers as part of the major or primary operations of the business; may occur as inflows of assets or decreases in liabilities.

26. The excess of expenses over revenues for a period.

27. The accounting principle that requires financial statement information to be based on actual costs incurred in business transactions; it requires assets and services to be recorded initially at the cash or cash equivalent amount given in exchange.

28. The rule that provides guidance on when revenue should be reflected on the income statement; the rule includes three guidelines (1) requires revenue to be recognized at the time it is earned, (2) allows the inflow of assets associated with revenue to be in a form other than cash, and (3) measures the amount of revenue as the cash plus the cash equivalent value of any noncash assets received from customers in exchange for goods or services.

29. The rules adopted by the accounting profession as guides for conducting audits of financial statements.

30. A liability created by buying goods or services on credit.

31. The owner's claim on the assets of a business; more precisely, the residual interest in the assets of an entity that remains after deducting its liabilities; also called *net assets*.

32. Properties or economic resources owned by the business; more precisely, resources with an ability to provide future benefits to the business.

33. International Accounting Standards Committee; a committee that attempts to create more harmony among the accounting practices of different countries by identifying preferred practices and encouraging their worldwide acceptance.

34. Individuals or organizations that owe amounts to a business.

35. The excess of revenues over expenses for a period.

36. Auditing Standards Board: the authoritative committee that identifies generally accepted auditing standards.

37. The rules adopted by the accounting profession that make up acceptable accounting practices for the preparation of financial statements.

38. Outflows or the using up of assets as a result of the major or central operations of a business; also, liabilities may be increased.

39. Distributiblack

40. Black

41. ons of assets by a corporation to its owners.

42. Another name for the *going-concern principle*.

43. An asset created by selling products or services on credit.

Problem IV

Complete the following by filling in the blanks.

1. Expenses are outflows or the _____ of assets as a result of the major or central operations of a business.

2. Assets created by selling goods and services on credit are called _____.
    Liabilities created by buying goods and services on credit are called _____.

3. The balance sheet equation is _____ equals _____ plus _____. It is also called the _____ equation.

4. An excess of revenues over expenses for a period results in a _____. An excess of expenses over revenues results in a _____. The financial statement that lists revenues and expenses is the _____.

5. A balance sheet prepared for a business shows its financial position as of a specific _____. Financial position is shown by listing the _____ of the business, its _____, and its _____.

6. Equity on a balance sheet is the difference between a company's _____ and its _____.

7. Probable future sacrifices of economic benefits arising from present obligations of a particular entity to transfer assets or provide services to other entities in the future as a result of past transactions or events are called _____.

8. Individuals or organizations entitled to receive payment from a company are called _____ and those owing money to a business are called _____.

9. Under the _____ principle every business is to be accounted for as a separate entity separate and distinct from its _____ or _____.

10. The statement of cash flows shows the events that caused _____ to change. It classifies the cash flow into three major categories: _____, _____, and _____ activities.

11. The statement of owner's equity discloses all changes in equity during the period including _____, _____, and _____.

12. The cost principle requires financial statement information to be based on _____ incurred in business transactions. The going-concern principle requires financial statements to reflect the assumption that the business will _____ instead of being _____ or _____. The revenue recognition principle requires that revenue be recognized at the time it is _____.

Problem V

The assets, liabilities, and owner's equity of Josie Long's computer consulting business are shown on the first line in the equation below, and following the equation are eight transactions completed by Ms. Long. Show by additions and subtractions in the spaces provided the effects of each transaction on the items of the equation. Show new totals after each transaction as in Illustration 2-14 in the text.

	Cash	+ Accounts Receivable +	Prepaid Rent	+ Computer Equipment +	Office Equipment =	Accounts Payable +	J. Long, Capital
	$5,000			$8,000	$6,300		$19,300
1.	-2,700		+$2,700				
	$2,300		$2,700				
2.	-850				+850		
	$1,450		$2,700		$7,150		
3.	+2,200						+2,200
	$3,650			$8,200			$21,500
4.				+650		+650	
				$8,650		$650	
5.		+$1,500					+1,500
		$1,500					$23,000
6.	-650					-650	
	$7,000					-0-	
7.	+1,500	-1,500					
	$4,500	-0-					
8.	-650						-650
	$3,850						$22,350

1. Paid the rent for three months in advance on the business office, $2,700.
2. Paid cash to purchase a new telephone for the office, $850.
3. Completed consulting work for John Lee and immediately collected the full payment of $2,200 in cash.
4. Purchased computer equipment on credit, $650.
5. Completed $1,500 of computer work for Ray Block on credit, and immediately entered in the accounting records both the right to collect and the revenue earned.
6. Paid for the computer equipment purchased in Transaction 4.
7. Received $1,500 from Ray Block for the consulting work in Transaction 5.
8. Paid the weekly salary of the assistant, $650.

Refer to your completed equation and fill in the blanks:

a. Did each transaction affect two items of the equation? _____

b. Did the equation remain in balance after the effects of each transaction were entered? _____

c. If the equation had not remained in balance after the effects of each transaction were entered, this would have indicated that _____.

Fundamental Accounting Principles, 10th Canadian Edition

d. Ms. Long earned $2,200 of revenue upon the completion of Transaction 3, and the asset that flowed into the business as a result of this transaction was in the form of _____.

e. Ms. Long earned $1,500 of revenue upon the completion of Transaction 5, and the asset that flowed into the business upon the completion of this transaction was _____.

f. The right to collect $1,500 from Ray Block was converted into _____ in Transaction 7. Nevertheless, the revenue was earned upon the completion of the _____ in Transaction 5.

g. The $1,500 collected in Transaction 7 was recognized as revenue in Transaction 5 because of the _____ principle, which states that (1) revenue should be recognized at the time it is _____; (2) the inflow of assets associated with revenue may be in a form other than _____; and (3) the amount of revenue should be measured as the cash plus the cash equivalent value of any _____ received from customers in exchange for goods or services.

Solutions for Chapter 2

Problem I

1. F
2. T
3. F
4. F
5. T

Problem II

1. B
2. B
3. D
4. B
5. E

Problem III

Problem IV

1. using up (consuming)
2. accounts receivable; accounts payable
3. Assets; Liabilities; Owner's Equity; accounting
4. net income (profit); net loss; income statement
5. date; assets; liabilities; equity
6. assets; liabilities
7. liabilities
8. creditors; debtors
9. business entity; owner; owners
10. cash, operating; investing; financing
11. net income or net loss; new investments by the owner; withdrawals
12. costs; going-concern; continuing concern; earned

Problem V

	Cash	Accounts + Receivable +	Prepaid Rent	Computer + Equipment +	Office Equipment =	Accounts Payable +	J. Long, Capital
						Liabilities +	Owner's Equity
	$5,000			$8,000	$6,300		$19,300
1.	−2,700		+2,700				
	$2,300		$2,700	$8,000	$6,300		$19,300
2.	−850				+850		
	$1,450		$2,700	$8,000	$7,150		$19,300
3.	+2,200						+2,200
	$3,650		$2,700	$8,000	$7,150		$21,500
4.				+200		+200	
	$3,650		$2,700	$8,200	$7,150	$200	$21,500
5.		+1,500					+1,500
	$3,650	$1,500	$2,700	$8,200	$7,150	$200	$23,000
6.	−200					−200	
	$3,450	$1,500	$2,700	$8,200	$7,150	$ -0-	$23,000
7.	+1,500	−1,500					
	$4,950	$ -0-	$2,700	$8,200	$7,150	$ -0-	$23,000
8.	−600						−600
	$4,350	$ -0-	$2,700	$8,200	$7,150	$ -0-	$22,400

a. Yes

b. Yes

c. an error had been made

d. cash

e. an account receivable

f. cash; legal work

g. revenue recognition (or realization); earned; cash; noncash assets

CHAPTER 3
ANALYZING AND RECORDING TRANSACTIONS

Learning Objective 1:

Explain the accounting cycle.

Summary

The steps in preparing financial statements for users repeated each reporting period.

Learning Objective 2:

Explain the steps in processing transactions.

Summary

The accounting cycle captures business transactions and events, analyzes and records their effects, and summarizes and prepares information useful in making decisions. Transactions and events are the starting points in the accounting cycle. Source documents help in analyzing them. The effects of transactions and events are recorded in the accounting books. Postings and the trial balance help summarize and classify these effects. The final step is providing this information in useful reports or financial statements to decision makers.

Learning Objective 3:

Describe source documents and their purpose.

Summary

Source documents are business papers that identify and describe transactions and events. Examples are sales invoices, cheques, purchase orders, bills, and bank statements. Source documents help ensure accounting records include all transactions. They also help prevent mistakes and theft, and are important to internal control. Source documents provide objective evidence making information more reliable and useful.

Learning Objective 4:

Describe an account and its use in recording information about transactions.

Summary

An account is a detailed record of increases and decreases in a specific asset, liability, or equity item. Information is taken from accounts, analyzed, summarized, and presented in useful reports and financial statements for users.

Learning Objective 5:

Describe a ledger and a chart of accounts.

Summary

A ledger is a record containing all accounts used by a company. This is what is referred to as *the books*. The chart of accounts is a listing of all accounts and usually includes an identification number assigned to each account.

Learning Objective 6:

Define debits and credits and explain their role in double-entry accounting.

Summary

Debit refers to left, and credit refers to right. Debits increase assets, withdrawals and expenses, while credits decrease them. Credits increase liabilities, capital and revenues, while debits decrease them. Double-entry accounting means every transaction affects at least two accounts. The total amount debited must equal the total amount credited for each transaction. The system for recording debits and credits follows from the accounting equation. The debit side is the normal balance for assets, owner's withdrawals, and expenses, and the credit side is the normal balance for liabilities, owner's capital, and revenues.

Learning Objective 7:

Analyze the impact of transactions on accounts.

Summary

We analyze transactions using the concepts of double-entry accounting. This analysis is performed by determining a transaction's effects on accounts. These effects are recorded in journals and posted to accounts in the ledger.

Learning Objective 8:

Record transactions in a journal and post entries to a ledger.

Summary

We record transactions in a journal to give a record of their effects. Each entry in a journal is posted to the accounts in the ledger. This provides information in accounts that is used to produce financial statements. Balance column ledger accounts are widely used and include columns for debits, credits and the account balance after each entry.

Learning Objective 9:

Prepare and explain the use of a trial balance.

Summary

A trial balance is a list of accounts in the ledger showing the debit and credit balances in separate columns. The trial balance is a convenient summary of the ledger's contents and is useful in preparing financial statements. It reveals errors of the kind that produce unequal debit and credit account balances.

Chapter Outline

I.   The Accounting Cycle

  A. Refers to the steps in preparing financial statements for users. The steps are repeated each reporting period. The steps are: analyze transactions, journalize, post, prepared unadjusted trial balance, adjust, prepare adjusted trial balance, prepare statements, close, and prepared post-closing trial balance.

II.   Transactions and Documents

  A. Relies on source documents
      Source documents identify and describe transactions and events entering the business process. Examples are sales invoices, cheques, purchase orders, charges to customers, bills from suppliers, employee earnings records, and bank statements. Source documents provide objective evidence about transactions, making information more reliable and useful.

  B. Analyze transactions and events using the accounting equation to understand how they affect organization performance and financial position.

  C. Record, summarize and classify the effects in the accounting books.

III. Accounts and Double-Entry Accounting

  A. *An account* is a detailed record of increases and decreases in a specific asset, liability, or equity item.

  B. Separate accounts are kept for each type of asset, liability, and equity item. Examples of the different types of accounts are:

    1. *Assets:* are resources controlled by an organization that have current and future benefits. They have value and are used in the operations of the business to create revenue. Some asset accounts are:

        a. Cash: includes money and any form of exchange that a bank accepts for deposit.

        b. Accounts Receivables: recorded when services are performed for or goods are sold to customers in return for promises to pay in the future, transactions are *on credit* or *on account*.

        c. Note Receivable: or promissory note: an unconditional written promise to pay a definite sum of money on demand or on a defined future date.

      d.   Prepaid Expenses: asset account containing payments made for assets that are not used until later. As these assets are used up, the costs of the used assets become expenses. Examples are supplies, prepaid insurance, prepaid rent, and advance payments for services.

      e.   Equipment: Assets used in a business, such as computers, furniture, counters, and showcases.

      f.   Buildings: Space provided for use as a store, office, warehouse, or factory.

      g.   Land: Cost is separated from the cost of buildings to provide more useful information

2.   *Liabilities:* are obligations to transfer assets or provide services to other entities. Some asset accounts are:

      a.   Accounts payable: produced when purchases are made by a promise to pay later.

      b.   Note payable: when an organization formally recognizes a promise to pay by signing a promissory note.

      c.   Unearned revenues: a liability that is satisfied by delivering products or services in the future.

3.   *Equity accounts:* include:

      a.   Owner's capital: owner's investments recorded in an account identified by the owner's name and the title *Capital*.

      b.   Owner's withdrawals: an account with the owner's name and the word *Withdrawals*.

      c.   Revenues and Expenses: revenues earned and expenses incurred for a period.

C. *The ledger*, is a record containing of all accounts used by a business. The *chart of accounts* is a list of all accounts used by a company.

D. A T-account is an informal tool used in showing the effects of transactions and events on specific accounts. Its shape looks like the letter T. The format includes:

1.   The account title on top, the left or debit side (*Dr.*), and the right or credit side (*Cr.*).

2.   *Liabilities*: Accounts Payable, Notes Payable, and Unearned Revenues.

3.   *Equity:* Owner's Capital, Owner's Withdrawals, Revenues and Expenses.

Chapter Outline

            4. A T-account provides one side for recording in increases in the item and the other side for decreases. An account balance is the difference between the increases and decreases recorded in an account.

    E. Double-entry accounting means every transaction affects and is recorded in at least two accounts. *The total amount debited must equal the total amount credited.* Therefore, the sum of the debits for all entries must equal the sum of the credits for all entries. The sum of the debit account balances must equal the sum of the credit account balances.

    F. The system for recording debits and credits balances follows the accounting equation. The *normal* balance of each account refers to the debit or credit side where increases are recorded.

            1. *Assets* are on the *left side* of the equation; therefore the left or *debit* side is the normal balance for assets. Increases in assets are debited to asset accounts. Decreases in assets are credited to asset accounts.

            2. *Liabilities and owner's equity* are on the *right* side; therefore the right or the *credit* side is the normal balance for liabilities and equity. Increases in liabilities and owner's equity are credited, and decreases are debited.

            3. *Owner's Investments, Owner's Withdrawals, revenues, and expenses* are changes in owner's equity. Owner's Investments and Revenues increase owner's equity, and are credited. *Withdrawals and expense* accounts decrease owner's equity, and are debited.

IV.   Analyzing Transactions

Step one: analyze a transaction and its source document(s).

Step two: Apply double-entry accounting to identify the effect of a transaction on account balances.

V.   Recording and Posting Transactions

A. *Journalizing* is the process of recording transactions in a journal. Recording transactions in a journal avoid the potential for error and the difficulty in tracking mistakes. A *general journal* gives a complete record of each transaction in one place, linking directly the debits and credits for each transaction.

B. *Posting* is the process of transferring journal entry information from the journal to the ledger. *This step occurs only after debits and credits for each transaction are entered into a journal.*

VI.   Trial Balance

A. A trial balance is a list of accounts and their balances at a point in time. Account balances are reported in the debit or credit columns. The sum of debit account balances must equal the sum of credit account balances.

B. One purpose for preparing a trial balance is to test for the equality of the debit and credit account balances. Another reason is to simplify the task of preparing the financial statements.

C. When a trial balance does not balance, one or more errors exist (the columns are not equal), at least one error has occurred in one of the following steps:

1.   preparing journal entries

2.   posting entries to the ledger

3.   computing account balances

4.   copying account balances to the trial balance

5.   totalling the trial balance columns.

Any errors must be found and corrected before preparing the financial statements.

THREE PARTS OF AN ACCOUNT

(1) ACCOUNT TITLE	
Left Side	Right Side
Called	called
(2) DEBIT	(3) CREDIT

Rules for using accounts

Accounts have <u>balance</u> sides (Debit or Credit)

To <u>increase</u> any account, use the balance side

To <u>decrease</u> any account, use the <u>side opposite</u> the balance

Finding account balances

If total debits = total credits, the account balance is zero.

If total <u>debits are greater</u> than total credits, the account has a <u>debit balance</u> equal to the difference of the two totals.

If total <u>credits are greater</u> than total debits, the account has a <u>credit balance</u> equal to the difference of the two totals.

REAL ACCOUNTS

ALL ACCOUNTS HAVE BALANCE SIDES

BALANCE SIDES FOR ASSETS, LIABILITIES, AND
EQUITY ACCOUNTS ARE BASED ON
THE SIDE OF <u>EQUATION</u> THEY ARE ON.

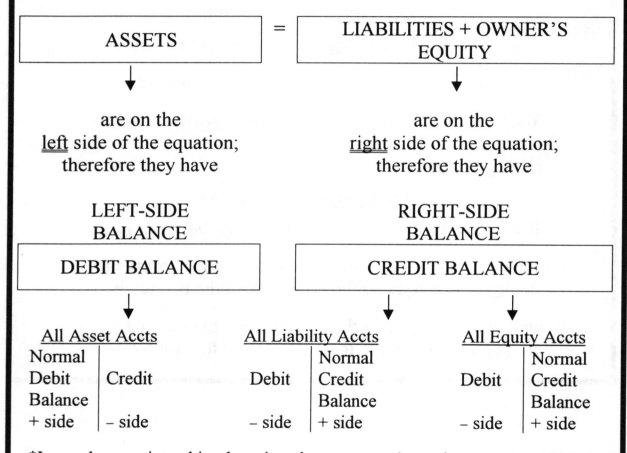

ASSETS	=	LIABILITIES + OWNER'S EQUITY

are on the
<u>left</u> side of the equation;
therefore they have

are on the
<u>right</u> side of the equation;
therefore they have

LEFT-SIDE
BALANCE

RIGHT-SIDE
BALANCE

DEBIT BALANCE	CREDIT BALANCE

<u>All Asset Accts</u>

Normal Debit Balance + side	Credit – side

<u>All Liability Accts</u>

Debit – side	Normal Credit Balance + side

<u>All Equity Accts</u>

Debit – side	Normal Credit Balance + side

*In a sole proprietorship, there is only one owner's equity account, which is called capital. For that reason, the terms equity and capital are often used interchangeably. When corporations are discussed in detail, you will learn many (shareholder's) equity accounts. Owner's equity is an account classification like assets. Owner's name, capital, is the account title.

Fundamental Accounting Principles, 10th Canadian Edition

Problem I

The following statements are either true or false. Place a (T) in the parentheses before each true statement and an (F) before each false statement.

1. ( ) Credits are used to record increases in assets, withdrawals, and expenses.

2. ( ) The process of recording transactions in a journal is called posting.

3. ( ) In double-entry accounting, all errors are avoided by being sure that debits and credits are equal when transactions are recorded.

4. ( ) The cost of renting an office during the current period is an expense; however, the cost of renting an office six periods in advance is an asset.

5. ( ) Liability accounts include accounts payable, unearned revenues, and equipment.

Problem II

You are given several words, phrases, or numbers to choose from in completing each of the following statements or in answering the following questions. In each case select the one that best completes the statement or answers the question, and place its letter in the answer space provided.

_____ 1. Leo Foreman's company had a capital balance of $23,400 on June 30 and $28,600 on July 31. Net income for the month of July was $15,000. How much did Foreman withdraw from the business during July?

 a. $5,200.

 b. $9,800.

 c. $15,000.

 d. $20,200.

 e. $0.

_____ 2. Which of the following transactions does not affect the owner's equity in a proprietorship?

 a. Investments by the owner.

 b. Withdrawals of cash by the owner.

 c. Cash receipts for revenues.

 d. Cash receipts for unearned revenues.

 e. Cash payments for expenses.

_____ 3. A ledger is:

 a. A book of original entry in which the effects of transactions are first recorded.

 b. The collection of all accounts used by a business.

 c. A book of original entry in which any type of transaction can be recorded.

 d. A book of special journals.

 e. An account with debit and credit columns and a third column for showing the balance of the account.

_____ 4. The following transactions occurred during the month of October:

    1) Paid $1,500 cash for store equipment.

    2) Paid $1,000 in partial payment for supplies purchased 30 days previously.

    3) Paid October's utility bill of $600.

    4) Paid $1,200 to owner of business for his personal use.

    5) Paid $1,400 salary of office employee for October.

What was the total amount of expenses during October?

  a. $3,000.

  b. $4,500.

  c. $2,000.

  d. $3,500.

  e. $5,700.

_____ 5. The journal entry to record the completion of legal work for a client on credit and billing the client $1,700 for the services rendered would be:

  a. Accounts Receivable 1,700

        Unearned Legal Fees..   1,700

  b. Legal Fees Earned 1,700

        Accounts Receivable   1,700

  c. Accounts Payable 1,700

        Legal Fees Earned   1,700

  d. Legal Fees Earned.. 1,700

        Sales   1,700

  e. Accounts Receivable 1,700

        Legal Fees Earned..   1,700

Problem III

Following are the first ten transactions completed by A. P. Larsen's new business called Larsen's Repair Shop:

    a.   Started the business with a cash deposit of $4,000 to a bank account in the name of the business.

    b.   Paid three months' rent in advance on the shop space, $1,500.

    c.   Purchased repair equipment for cash, $2,200.

    d.   Completed repair work for customers and collected cash, $1,200.

    e.   Purchased additional repair equipment on credit from Lenney Company, $575.

    f.   Completed repair work on credit for Joe Whalen, $250.

    g.   Paid Lenney Company $300 of the amount owed from transaction (e).

    h.   Paid the local radio station $150 for an announcement of the shop opening.

    i.   Joe Whalen paid for the work completed in transaction (f).

    j.   Withdrew $350 cash from the bank for A. P. Larsen to pay personal expenses.

Required

1.   Record the transactions directly in the T-accounts that follow. Use the transaction letters to identify the amounts in the accounts.

2.   Prepare a trial balance as of the current date using the form that follows.

Cash	Accounts Payable
	A. P. Larsen, Capital
Accounts Receivable	A. P. Larsen, Withdrawals
Prepaid Rent	Repair Services Revenue
Repair Equipment	Advertising Expense

Trial Balance

_____, 19____

Problem IV

Journalize the following transactions and post to the accounts that follow.

a. On November 5 of the current year, Megan Lear invested $1,700 in cash, and equipment having a fair value of $800, to start a decorating business.

b. On November 6, the business purchased additional equipment for $425 cash.

GENERAL JOURNAL

DATE	ACCOUNT TITLES ANDEXPLANATION	P.R.	DEBIT	CREDIT

GENERAL LEDGER

Cash   Account No. 101

DATE	EXPLANATION	P.R.	DEBIT	CREDIT

Equipment   Account No. 163

DATE	EXPLANATION	P.R.	DEBIT	CREDIT

Megan Lear, Capital   Account No. 301

DATE	EXPLANATION	P.R.	DEBIT	CREDIT

Problem V

Many of the important ideas and concepts discussed in Chapter 3 are reflected in the following list of key terms. Test your understanding of these terms by matching the appropriate definition with the terms. Record the number identifying the most appropriate definition in the blank space next to each term.

_____ Account	_____ Journalizing
_____ Account balance	_____ Normal balance
_____ Accounting cycle	_____ Ledger
_____ Balance column ledger account	_____ Note Receivable
_____ Chart of accounts	_____ Posting
_____ Compound journal entry	_____ Posting Reference (PR) column
_____ Credit	_____ Prepaid expenses
_____ Debit	_____ Promissory Note
_____ Double-entry accounting	_____ Source documents
_____ External transactions	_____ T-account
_____ General Journal	_____ Trial balance
_____ Internal transactions	_____ Unearned revenues
_____ Journal	

1. The most flexible type of journal; can be used to record any kind of transaction.

2. An asset account containing payments made for assets that are not used until later.

3. The steps repeated each reporting period for the purpose of preparing financial statements for users.

4. A list of accounts and their balances at a point in time; the total debit balances should equal the total credit balances.

5. The debit or credit side on which an account increases

6. A place or location within an accounting system in which the increases and decreases in a specific asset, liability, or equity are recorded and stored.

7. A list of all accounts used by a company; includes the identification number assigned to each account.

8. An unconditional written promise to pay a definite sum of money on demand or on a defined future date(s); also called note receivable.

9. Liabilities created when customers pay in advance for products or services; created when cash is received before revenues are earned; satisfied by delivering the products or services in the future.

10. A record where transactions are recorded before they are recorded in accounts; amounts are posted from the journal to the ledger; also called the book of original entry.

11. A journal entry that affects at least three accounts.

12. An account with debit and credit columns for recording entries and a third column for showing the balance of the account after each entry is posted.

13. An unconditional written promise to pay a definite sum of money on demand or on a defined future date(s); also called promissory note.

14. A column in journals where individual account numbers are entered when entries are posted to the ledger. A column in ledgers where journal page numbers are entered when entries are posted.

15. The process of recording transactions in a journal.

16. An entry that increases asset, expense, and owner's withdrawals accounts or decreases liability, owner's capital, and revenue accounts; recorded on the left side of a T-account.

17. The process of transferring journal entry information to ledger accounts.

18. A simple characterization of an account form used as a helpful tool in showing the effects of transactions and events on specific accounts.

19. An entry that decreases asset, expenses, and owner's withdrawals accounts or increases liability, owner's capital, and revenue accounts; recorded on the right side of a T-account.

20. The difference between the increases (including the beginning balance) and decreases recorded in an account.

21. These are the source of information recorded with accounting entries and can be in either paper or electronic form.

22. An accounting system where every transaction affects and is recorded in at least two accounts; the sum of the debits for all entries must equal the sum of the credits for all entries.

23. A record containing all accounts used by a business.

24. Exchanges between the entity and some other person or organization.

25. Exchanges within an organization that can also affect the accounting equation.

Problem VI

Complete the following by filling in the blanks.

1. Assets are resources controlled by an organization that have _____ and _____ benefits. They have value and are used in the operations of the business to create _____ .

2. A _____ is an amount of cash that the business is expecting to receive in the future. When services are performed for or goods are sold to customers in return for promises to pay in the future, a(n) _____ is recorded. A _____ , or a _____ , is an unconditional written promise to pay a definite sum of money on demand or on a defined future date.

3. A _____ is an obligation to transfer assets or provide services to other entities. Purchases of merchandise, supplies, equipment or services made by an oral or implied promise to pay later produce _____ _____ . _____ _____ is satisfied by delivering products or services in the future.

4. Four transactions that affect equity are _____ , _____ , _____ , and _____ .

5. The process of recording transactions in a journal is called _____ . The process of transferring journal entry information to the ledger is called _____ .

6. The _____ creates a link between a journal entry and the ledger accounts by providing a cross-reference for tracing the entry from one record to the other.

7. Notes receivable and prepaid insurance are examples of a(n) _____ account. Unearned revenues and interest payable are examples of a(n) _____ account.

8. Balances of _____ and _____ accounts flow into the income statement. Then, net income from the income statement and balances from _____ and _____ accounts flow into the statement of changes in owner's equity. Then, ending owner's equity and balances from _____ and _____ accounts flow into the balance sheet.

9. a. The normal balance of an asset account is a _____.

    b. The normal balance of a liability account is a _____.

    c. The normal balance of the capital account is a _____.

    d. The normal balance of the withdrawals account is _____.

    e. The normal balance of a revenue account is a _____.

    f. The normal balance of an expense account is a _____.

10. The steps in preparing a trial balance are: _____

    _____

    _____

    _____

    _____

    _____

    _____

    _____

    _____

11. A trial balance that balances is not absolute proof that no errors were made because

    _____.

12. One frequent error that is made is called a _____, which occurs when two digits within a number are switched. This type of error probably has occurred if the difference between the two trial balance columns is evenly divisible by _____.

Solutions for Chapter 3

Problem I

1. F
2. F
3. F
4. T
5. F

Problem II

1. B
2. D
3. B
4. C
5. E

Problem III

	Cash		
(a)	4,000.00	(b)	1,500.00
(d)	1,200.00	(c)	2,200.00
(i)	250.00	(g)	300.00
		(h)	150.00
		(j)	350.00

	Repair Equipment	
(c)	2,200.00	
(e)	575.00	

	A. P. Larsen, Withdrawals	
(j)	350.00	

	Accounts Receivable		
(f)	250.00	(i)	250.00

	Accounts Payable		
(g)	300.00	(e)	575.00

	Repair Services Revenue		
		(d)	1,200.00
		(f)	250.00

	Prepaid Rent	
(b)	1,500.00	

	A. P. Larsen, Capital		
		(a)	4,000.00

	Advertising Expense	
(h)	150.00	

LARSEN'S REPAIR SHOP
Trial Balance
(Current Date)

Cash	$ 950.00	
Prepaid rent	1,500.00	
Repair equipment	2,775.00	
Accounts payable		$ 275.00
P. L. Wheeler, capital		4,000.00
P. L. Wheeler, withdrawals	350.00	
Repair services revenue		1,450.00
Advertising expense	150.00	
Totals	$5,725.00	$5,725.00

Problem IV

GENERAL JOURNAL

DATE	ACCOUNT TITLES AND EXPLANATION	P.R.	DEBIT	CREDIT
19— Nov. 5	Cash	101	1 7 0 0 00	
	Equipment	163	8 0 0 00	
	Megan Lear, Capital	301		2 5 0 0 00
	Owner's initial investment.			
6	Equipment	163	4 2 5 00	
	Cash	101		4 2 5 00
	Purchased office equipment			

GENERAL LEDGER

Cash   Account No. 101

DATE	EXPLANATION	P.R.	DEBIT	CREDIT	BALANCE
19— Nov. 5		G-1	1 7 0 0 00		1 7 0 0 00
6		G-1		4 2 5 00	1 2 7 5 00

Equipment   Account No. 163

DATE	EXPLANATION	P.R.	DEBIT	CREDIT	BALANCE
19— Nov. 5		G-1	8 0 0 00		8 0 0 00
6		G-1	4 2 5 00		1 2 2 5 00

Megan Lear, Capital   Account No. 301

DATE	EXPLANATION	P.R.	DEBIT	CREDIT	BALANCE
19— Nov. 5		G-1		2 5 0 0 00	2 5 0 0 00

Problem V

Problem VI

1. current, future, revenue

2. receivable, account receivable, note receivable, promissory note

3. liability, account payable, unearned revenue

4. investment by the owner, withdrawals by the owner, revenues, expenses

5. journalizing, posting

6. Posting Reference (PR) column

7. asset, liability

8. revenue, expense; capital, withdrawals; asset, liability

9. (a) debit; (b) credit; (c) credit; (d) debit; (e) credit; (f) debit

10. (1) Determine the balance of each account; (2) List in their ledger order the accounts having balances, with the debit balances in one column and the credit balances in another; (3) Add the debit balances; (4) Add the credit balances; (5) Compare the two totals for equality.

11. some types of errors do not create unequal debits and credits

12. transposition, nine

CHAPTER 4
ADJUSTING ACCOUNTS FOR FINANCIAL STATEMENTS

Learning Objective 1:

Describe the purpose of adjusting accounts at the end of a period.

Summary

After external transactions are recorded, several accounts in the ledger often need adjusting for their balances to appear correctly in financial statements. This need arises because internal transactions and events remain unrecorded. The purpose of adjusting accounts at the end of a period is to recognize revenues earned and expenses incurred during the period that are not yet recorded.

Learning Objective 2:

Explain the importance of periodic reporting and the time period principle.

Summary

The value of information is often linked to its timeliness. Useful information must reach decision makers frequently and promptly. To provide timely information, accounting systems prepare periodic reports at regular intervals. The time period principle assumes that an organization's activities can be divided into specific time periods such as a month, a three-month quarter, or a year for periodic reporting.

Learning Objective 3:

Explain accrual accounting and how it adds to the usefulness of financial statements.

Summary

Accrual accounting recognizes revenue when earned and expenses when incurred. Accrual accounting reports the economic effects of events when they occur, not necessarily when cash inflows and outflows occur. This information is viewed as valuable in assessing a company's financial position and performance.

Learning Objective 4:

Identify the types of adjustments and their purpose.

Summary

Adjustments can be grouped according to their timing of cash receipts or payments relative to when they are recognized as revenues or expenses. There are 2 major groups, *prepaids/unearned* and *accruals*. Both of these can be subdivided into expenses and revenues. Adjusting entries are necessary for each of these groups so that revenues, expenses, assets and liabilities are correctly reported for each period.

Learning Objective 5:

Prepare and explain adjusting entries for prepaid expenses, amortization and unearned revenues.

Summary

Prepaid expenses refer to items paid for in advance of receiving their benefits. Prepaid expenses are assets. As this asset is used, its cost becomes an expense. Adjusting entries for prepaids involve increasing (debiting) expenses and decreasing (crediting) assets. Amortization is the expense created by spreading the cost of capital assets over the periods these assets are used. Accumulated amortization, a contra asset account, is credited to track the total amount of the capital asset used. Unearned (or prepaid) revenues refer to cash received in advance of providing products and services. Unearned revenues are a liability. As products and services are provided, the amount of unearned revenues becomes earned revenues. Adjusting entries for unearned revenues involve increasing (crediting) revenues and decreasing (debiting) unearned revenues.

Learning Objective 6:

Prepare and describe adjusting entries for accrued expenses and accrued revenues.

Summary

Accrued expenses refer to costs incurred in a period that are both unpaid and unrecorded. Accrued expenses are part of expenses and reported on the income statement. Adjusting entries for recording accrued expenses involve increasing (debiting) expenses and increasing (crediting) liabilities. Accrued revenues refer to revenues earned in a period that are both unrecorded and not yet received in cash. Accrued revenues are part of revenues and reported on the income statement. Adjusting entries for recording accrued revenues involve increasing (debiting) assets and increasing (crediting) revenues.

Learning Objective 7:

Explain how accounting adjustments link to financial statements.

Summary

Accounting adjustments bring an asset or liability account balance to its correct amount. They also update related expense or revenue accounts. Every adjusting entry affects one or more income statement accounts and one or more balance sheet accounts. An adjusting entry never affects cash. Adjustments are necessary for transactions and events that extend over more than one period. Exhibit 4.20 summarizes financial statement links by type of adjustment.

Learning Objective 8:

Explain and prepare an adjusted trial balance.

Summary

An adjusted trial balance is a list of accounts and balances prepared after adjusting entries are recorded and posted to the ledger. Financial statements are often prepared from the adjusted trial balance.

Learning Objective 9:

Prepare financial statements from an adjusted trial balance.

Summary

We can prepare financial statements directly from the adjusted trial balance that includes all account balances. Revenue and expense balances are transferred to the income statement and statement of owner's equity. Asset, liability and owner's equity balances are transferred to the balance sheet. We usually prepare statements in the following order: income statement, statement of owner's equity, and balance sheet.

Learning Objective 10:

Record and describe entries for later periods that result from accruals.

Summary

Accrued revenues at the end of one accounting period usually result in cash receipts from customers in later periods. Accrued expenses at the end of one accounting period usually result in cash payments in later periods. When cash is received or paid in these later periods, the entries must account for the accrued assets or liabilities initially recorded.

Learning Objective 11 (Appendix 4A):

Identify and explain two alternatives in accounting for prepaids.

Summary

It is acceptable to charge all prepaid expenses to expense accounts when they are purchased. When this is done, adjusting entries must transfer any unexpired amounts from expense accounts to asset accounts. It is also accept to credit all unearned revenues to revenue accounts when cash is received. In this case the adjusting entries must transfer any unearned amounts from revenue accounts to unearned revenue accounts.

Fundamental Accounting Principles, 10th Canadian Edition

Chapter Outline

I. Timing and Reporting

A. **Purpose of Adjusting**— At the end of the period, after external transactions are recorded, several accounts in the ledger need adjusting for their balances to appear in financial statements. This need arises because internal transactions and events remain unrecorded.

B. **The Accounting Period**—Time periods covered by statements.

1. Time period principle—assumes that an organization's activities can be divided into specific time periods such as a month, a three-month quarter, or a year.

2. The specific period a business adopts is its fiscal year—the 12 consecutive months selected as an organization's annual accounting period. The annual accounting period may be the:

   a. Calendar year—January 1 to December 31.

   b. Natural business year—a 12-month period that ends when a company's sales activities are at their lowest point.

C. **Recognizing Revenues and Expenses**—two main accounting principles are used, the revenue recognition principle and the matching principle:

1. The matching principle aims to report expenses in the same accounting period as the revenues that are earned as a result of the expenses.

D. **Accrual Basis Compared to Cash Basis**

1. Accrual basis accounting—revenues and expenses are recorded when earned or incurred regardless of when cash is received or paid. Based on GAAP.

2. Cash basis accounting—recognizes revenues and expenses when *cash* is received or paid. Not consistent with GAAP.

II. Adjusting Accounts—An adjusting entry is recorded to bring an asset or liability account balance to its proper amount when an adjustment is needed. This entry also updates the related expense or revenue account.

A. Framework for adjustments—amounts to adjust include prepaid expenses, amortization, unearned revenues, accrued expenses and accrued revenues.

Study Guide, Chapter 4

53

B. Adjusting Prepaid Expenses
    1. Prepaid expenses are items *paid for* in advance of receiving their benefits. Prepaid expenses are assets. As these assets are used, their costs become expenses.
    2. Common prepaid items: insurance, supplies, and amortization.
    3. Adjusting entries for prepaids involve increasing (debiting) expenses and decreasing (crediting) assets.

C. Adjusting for Amortization
    1. Capital assets include long-term tangible assets such as plant and equipment that are used to produce and sell products and services and, intangible assets such as patents that convey the right to use a product or process. These assets are expected to provide benefits for more than one period.
    2. Amortization is the process of computing expense from matching, or allocating, the cost of capital assets over their expected useful lives. Several methods can be used to calculate the amortization. With straight-line amortization method, cost of asset less estimated value at end of estimated useful life, divided by estimated useful life results in periodic amortization.
    3. Amortization is recorded in a contra account—an account linked with another account and having an opposite normal balance. The contra account for capital assets is called accumulated amortization. After posting the adjustment, the asset account balance less the contra account balance equals the balance sheet amount for this asset.

D. Adjusting Unearned Revenues
    1. Unearned Revenues are liabilities created when cash is received in advance of providing products and services.
    2. Adjusting entries for unearned revenues involve increasing (crediting) revenues and decreasing (debiting) unearned revenues.

E. Adjusting Accrued Expenses
    1. Accrued Expenses are costs incurred in a period that are both unpaid and unrecorded.
    2. Common accrued expenses are salaries, interest, rent and taxes.
    3. Adjusting entries for recording accrued expenses involve increasing (debiting) expenses and increasing (crediting) liabilities. (The liability is a "payable.")

      F. Adjusting Accrued Revenues

         1. Accrued Revenues are revenues earned in a period that are both unrecorded and not yet received in cash (or other assets).

         2. Commonly accrued revenues are fees for services and products, interest and rent.

         3. Adjusting entries increase (debit) assets and increase (credit) revenues. (The asset is a "receivable.")

      G. Adjustments and Financial Statements—each adjusting entry affects one or more income statement accounts *and* one or more balance sheet accounts. (See text exhibit 4.20 for a summary of adjustments and financial statement links. *Note that adjusting entries related to the framework never affect cash.*)

III.   **Adjusted Trial Balance—**

      A. Unadjusted trial balance—a list of accounts and balances prepared *before* adjustments are recorded.

      B. Adjusted trial balance—a list of accounts and balances prepared *after* adjusting entries are recorded and posted to the ledger.

IV.   **Preparing Financial Statements—**prepare financial statements directly from information in the *adjusted* trial balance. Because information flows from one statement to the next, prepare financial statements in the following order:

      A. Income Statement

      B. Statement of Owner's Equity (uses net income or loss from the income statement).

      C. Balance Sheet (uses ending equity from the statement of owner's equity). Balance Sheets can be prepared in one of two formats:

         1. Account form— lists assets on the left and liabilities and owner's equity on the right side of the balance sheet.

         2. Report form—lists items vertically, placing the assets above the liabilities and the owner's equity.

V.   **Accrual Adjustments in Later Periods—**accrued revenues/expenses of one period generally result in cash receipts/payments in next period.

      A. Paying accrued expenses—Debit the payable for amount previously accrued and credit cash for full amount paid. If the amount paid exceeds amount accrued, the difference is additional expense.

      B. Receiving accrued revenues—Debit cash for the full amount received and credit the receivable for amount previously accrued. If the amount received exceeds amount accrued, the difference is additional revenue.

Chapter Outline

VI. **Appendix 4A—Alternatives in accounting for Prepaids**

    A. Prepaid expenses may originally be recorded with debits to expense accounts instead of assets. If so, then adjusting entries must transfer the cost of the unused or unexpired portions from expense accounts to prepaid expense (asset) accounts.

    B. Prepaid revenues or revenues collected in advance may originally be recorded with credits to revenue accounts instead of liabilities. If so, then adjusting entries must transfer the unearned portions from revenue accounts to unearned revenue (liability) accounts.

    C. Note that the financial statements are identical under either procedure, but the adjusting entries are different.

ACCRUAL BASIS ACCOUNTING

(Follows GAAP)

requires that the

Income Statement (for a period)*

reports

GAAP Revenue Recognition

ALL REVENUES EARNED in period*(Collected or Not)

Minus ALL EXPENSES INCURRED in period* (Paid or Not)

Equals Net Income or Net Loss for the period*

GAAP Matching

GAAP *Periodicity

ACCOUNTS MUST BE ADJUSTED TO FOLLOW PRINCIPLES

UNEARNED/PREPAIDS

The converse of statements in Visual #5A also applies.
Results <u>Deferrals</u>*

UNEARNED = LIABILITY *

A REVENUE <u>not</u> earned, <u>cannot</u> be shown, even if collected.
An EXPENSE <u>not</u> incurred, <u>cannot</u> be shown, even if paid.

PREPAID = ASSET *

*We defer or postpone the <u>reporting</u> of the collected revenues
(as revenues) and prepaid expenses (as expenses) until the
revenue is earned and the expense is incurred.

ADJUSTMENTS		
TYPE	**GENERALIZED* ENTRY**	**AMOUNT**
1. Prepaid Items or Supplies a) initially recorded as assets	Dr. _____ Expense Cr. the Asset* acct.	Amount used, or consumed, or expired
b) initially recorded as expenses (alternate treatment)	Dr. the Asset** acct. Cr. _____ Expense	Amount left, or not consumed, unexpired
2. Amortization of capital assets	Dr. Amortization Expense Cr. Accumulated Amortization	Portion of cost of the asset allocated to this period as amortization
3. Unearned Revenues (revenues received in advance) a) initially recorded as a liability (Unearned Account)	Dr. Unearned _____ Cr. the Revenue** acct.	Amount earned to date
b) initially recorded as a revenue (alternate treatment)	Dr. the Revenue** acct. Cr. Unearned_____	Amount still <u>not</u> earned
2. Accrued Expenses (Expenses <u>incurred</u> but not yet recorded)	Dr. _____ Expense Cr. _____ Payable	Amount accrued
3. Accrued Revenues (Revenues <u>earned</u> but not yet recorded)	Dr. _____ Receivable Cr. the Revenue** acct.	Amount accrued

*Notice (1) Each adjustment affects a Balance Sheet Account and an Income Statement Account (2) <u>CASH</u> is <u>never</u> in an adjustment.

**Title or account name varies.

Problem I

The following statements are either true or false. Place a (T) in the parentheses before each true statement and an (F) before each false statement.

1. ( ) The effect of a debit to an unearned revenue account and a corresponding credit to a revenue account is to transfer the earned portion of the fee from the liability account to the revenue account.

2. ( ) If the accountant failed to make the end-of-period adjustment to remove from the Unearned Fees account the amount of fees earned, the omission would cause an overstatement of revenues.

3. ( ) The financial effect of a revenue generally occurs when it is earned, not when cash is received.

4. ( ) Under the accrual basis of accounting, revenues are recognized when they are earned and expenses are matched with revenues.

5. ( ) Amortizing capital assets causes the expense to be recorded when the asset is purchased.

Problem II

You are given several words, phrases, or numbers to choose from in completing each of the following statements or in answering the following questions. In each case select the one that best completes the statement or answers the question and place its letter in the answer space provided.

_____ 1. Time periods covered by statements are called:
   a. seasonal periods.
   b. fiscal years.
   c. operating cycles of a business.
   d. accounting periods.
   e. natural business years.

_____ 2. J Company paid in advance $300 for six months of insurance on the business. At the end of the first month, the journal entry to record the expense would be:

   a. Insurance Expense 300
         Cash   300
   b. Prepaid Insurance 300
         Cash   300
   c. Insurance Expense 50
         Prepaid Insurance   50
   d. Prepaid Insurance..50
         Insurance Expense   50
   e. No entry should be made until the salaries are actually paid.

_____ 3 During April of 2001, Sugee's Furniture received $250 cash in advance for future services. The following entry should be made when the money is received:

   a. Cash 250
         Accounts Receivable   250
   b. Accounts Receivable 250
         Unearned Revenue   250
   c. Cash...250
         Unearned Revenue   250
   d. Unearned Revenue 250
         Services Revenue   250
   e. No entry should be made until services are actually rendered.

_____ 4. On Dec. 1, B & B Security Service collected three months' fees of $6,000 in advance of providing services. The amount was recorded as a credit to Unearned Security Service Fees. They provided the monthly service from that date forward. The Dec. 31st adjustment will require Unearned Service Fees be

   a. Credited for $ 2,000.

   b. Debited for $ 6,000.

   c. Credited for $ 6,000.

   d. Debited for $ 4,000.

   e. Debited for $ 2,000.

_____ 5. Bud's Restaurant prepares monthly financial statements. On January 31 the balance in the Supplies account was $1,600. During February $2,960 of supplies were purchased and debited to Supplies. What is the adjusting entry on February 28 to account for the supplies assuming a February 28 inventory showed that $1,300 of supplies were on hand?

   a. Supplies Expense 300

       Supplies   300

   b. Supplies 300

       Supplies Expense   300

   c. Supplies 3,260

       Cash   3,260

   d. Supplies Expense 3,260

       Supplies   3,260

   e. Some other entry.

_____ 6. Jay's Delivery Services purchased equipment costing $15,000. The equipment was expected to have a useful life of 6 years. At the end of the 6 years, the equipment was expected to be sold for $3,000. Using straight-line amortization, the adjusting entry to amortize the equipment at the end of the first year would be:

   a. Amortization Expense...2,500

       Accumulated Amortization   2,500

   b. Amortization Expense...2,500

       Equipment   2,500

   c. Amortization Expense...2,000

       Accumulated Amortization   2,000

   d. Amortization Expense...2,000

       Equipment   2,000

   e. Some other entry.

Problem III

Many of the important ideas and concepts discussed in Chapter 4 are reflected in the following list of key terms. Test your understanding of these terms by matching the appropriate definitions with the terms. Record the number identifying the most appropriate definition in the blank space next to each term.

_____	Accounting form balance sheet	_____	Contra account
_____	Accounting period	_____	Intangible assets
_____	Accrual basis accounting	_____	Interim financial reports
_____	Accrued expenses	_____	Market value of an asset
_____	Accrued revenues	_____	Matching principle
_____	Adjusted trial balance	_____	Plant and equipment
_____	Adjusting entry	_____	Report form balance sheet
_____	Amortization	_____	Straight-line amortization method
_____	Book value of an asset	_____	Time-period principle
_____	Capital assets	_____	Unadjusted trial balance
_____	Cash basis accounting		

1. A journal entry at the end of an accounting period to bring an asset or liability account balance to its proper amount while also updating the related expense or revenue account.

2. A balance sheet that lists items vertically with assets above the liabilities and owner's equity.

3. Include long-term tangible assets, such as plant and equipment, and intangible assets, such as patents. These are expected to provide benefits for more than one period.

4. Long-lived (capital) assets that have no physical substance but convey a right to use a product or process.

5. An account linked with another account and having an opposite normal balance; reported as a subtraction from the other account's balance so that more complete information than simply the net amount is provided.

6. The approach to preparing financial statements that uses the adjusting process to recognize revenues when earned and expenses when incurred, not when cash is paid or received; the basis for generally accepted accounting principles.

7. Revenues earned in a period that are both unrecorded and not yet received in cash (or other asset); adjusting entries for recording accrued revenues involve increasing (debiting assets and increasing (crediting) revenues

8. A broad principle that assumes that an organization's activities can be divided into specific time periods such as months, quarter, or years.

9. The amount that an asset can be sold for; not tied to the book value of an asset.

10. A balance sheet that lists assets on the left and liabilities and owner's equity on the right side of the balance sheet.

11. The cost of the asset less its accumulated amortization.

12. A listing of accounts and balances prepared after adjustments are recorded and posted to the ledger.

13. The length of time covered by financial statements and other reports; also called reporting periods.

14.   The broad principle that requires expenses to be reported in the same period as the revenues that were earned as a result of the expenses.

15.   A listing of accounts and balances prepared before adjustments are recorded and posted to the ledger.

16.   The expense created by allocating the cost of plant and equipment to the periods in which they are used; represents the expense of using the assets.

17.   Costs incurred in a period that are both unpaid and unrecorded; adjusting entries for recording accrued expenses involve increasing (debiting) expenses and increasing (crediting) liabilities.

18.   Financial reports covering less than one year; usually based on one- or three- or six-month periods.

19.   Tangible long-lived assets used to produce goods or services.

20.   Revenues are recognized when cash is received and expenses are recorded when cash is paid.

21.   Allocates equal amounts of an asset's cost to amortization expense during its useful life.

Problem IV

On October 1 of the current year, George Lee began business repairing computers. During the month he completed the following transactions:

October   1   Invested $4,000 in the business.

           1   Paid three months' rent in advance on the office space, $1,545.

           1   Purchased office equipment for cash, $925.

           2   Purchased on credit office equipment, $700, and office supplies, $75.

         31   Completed repair work during the month and collected cash, $1,800. (Combined into one entry to conserve space.)

         31   Withdrew $800 for personal living expenses.

After the foregoing entries were recorded in the journal and posted, the accounts of George Lee appeared as follows:

GENERAL LEDGER

Cash   Account No. 101

DATE	EXPLANATION	P.R.	DEBIT	CREDIT	BALANCE
Oct. 1		G-1	4 0 0 0 00		4 0 0 0 00
1		G-1		1 5 4 5 00	2 4 5 5 00
1		G-1		9 2 5 00	1 5 3 0 00
31		G-2	1 8 0 0 00		3 3 3 0 00
31		G-2		8 0 0 00	2 5 3 0 00

Office Supplies   Account No. 124

DATE	EXPLANATION	P.R.	DEBIT	CREDIT	BALANCE
Oct. 2		G-1	7 5 00		7 5 00

Prepaid Rent   Account No. 131

DATE	EXPLANATION	P.R.	DEBIT	CREDIT	BALANCE
Oct. 1		G-1	1 5 4 5 00		1 5 4 5 00

Office Equipment — Account No. 163

DATE	EXPLANATION	P.R.	DEBIT	CREDIT	BALANCE
Oct. 1		G-1	9 2 5 00		9 2 5 00
2		G-1	7 0 0 00		1 6 2 5 00

Accumulated Amortization, Office Equipment — Account No. 164

DATE	EXPLANATION	P.R.	DEBIT	CREDIT	BALANCE

Accounts Payable — Account No. 201

DATE	EXPLANATION	P.R.	DEBIT	CREDIT	BALANCE
Oct. 2		G-1	7 7 5 00		7 7 5 00

George Lee, Capital — Account No. 301

DATE	EXPLANATION	P.R.	DEBIT	CREDIT	BALANCE
Oct. 1		G-1		4 0 0 0 00	4 0 0 0 00

George Lee, Withdrawals — Account No. 302

DATE	EXPLANATION	P.R.	DEBIT	CREDIT	BALANCE
Oct. 31		G-2	8 0 0 00		8 0 0 00

Repair Services Revenue — Account No. 403

DATE	EXPLANATION	P.R.	DEBIT	CREDIT	BALANCE
Oct. 31		G-2		1 8 0 0 00	1 8 0 0 00

	Amortization Expense, Office Equipment					Account No. 612
DATE	EXPLANATION	P.R.	DEBIT	CREDIT	BALANCE

	Rent Expense					Account No. 640
DATE	EXPLANATION	P.R.	DEBIT	CREDIT	BALANCE

	Office Supplies Expense					Account No. 650
DATE	EXPLANATION	P.R.	DEBIT	CREDIT	BALANCE

On October 31, George Lee decided to adjust his accounts and prepare a balance sheet and an income statement. His adjustments were:

a. One month's rent had expired.

b. An inventory of office supplies showed $40 of unused office supplies.

c. The office equipment had depreciated $35 during October.

Required:

1. Prepare and post general journal entries to record the adjustments.

2. After posting the adjusting entries, complete the adjusted trial balance.

3. From the adjusted trial balance complete the income statement, statement of owner's equity, and balance sheet.

DATE	ACCOUNT TITLES AND EXPLANATION	P.R.	DEBIT	CREDIT

GEORGE LEE

Adjusted Trial Balance

October 31, 2001

Account	P.R.	DEBIT	CREDIT
Cash			
Office supplies			
Prepaid rent			
Office equipment			
Accumulated amortization, office equipment			
Accounts payable			
George Lee, capital			
George Lee, withdrawals			
Repair services revenue			
Amortization expense, office equipment			
Rent expense			
Office supplies expense			
Totals			

GEORGE LEE

Income Statement

For Month Ended October 31, 2001

Revenue:			
Repair services revenue			
Operating expenses:			
Amortization expense, office equipment			
Rent expense			
Office supplies expense			
Total operating expenses			
Net income			

GEORGE LEE

Statement of Owner's Equity

For Month Ended October 31, 2001

George Lee, capital, October 1, 2001																		
October net income																		
Less withdrawals																		
Excess of income over withdrawals																		
George Lee, capital, October 31, 2001																		

GEORGE LEE

Balance Sheet

October 31, 2001

Assets																		
Cash																		
Office supplies																		
Prepaid rent																		
Office equipment																		
Less accumulated amortization																		
Total assets																		
Liabilities																		
Accounts payable																		
Owner's Equity																		
George Lee, capital, October 31, 2001																		
Total liabilities and owner's equity																		

Problem V

a. Long Company has one employee who earns $80.00 per day. The company operates with monthly accounting periods, and the employee is paid each Friday night for a workweek that begins on Monday. Assume the calendar for October appears as shown and enter the four $400.00 weekly salary payments directly in the T-accounts below. Then enter the adjustment for the wages earned but unpaid on October 31.

OCTOBER						
S	M	T	W	T	F	S
	1	2	3	4	5	6
7	8	9	10	11	12	13
14	15	16	17	18	19	20
21	22	23	24	25	26	27
28	29	30	31			

```
        Cash                Salaries Payable           Salaries Expense
_____|_____    _____|_____    _____|_____
               |                         |                          |
               |                         |                          |
               |                         |                          |
               |                         |                          |
```

b. Blade Company's October income statement should show $_____ of salaries expense, and its October 31 balance sheet should show a $_____ liability for salaries payable. The salaries earned by its employee but unpaid on October 31 are an example of an _____ expense.

c. In the space that follows give the general journal entry to record payment of a full week's wages to the Blade Company employee on November 2.

GENERAL JOURNAL   Page 1

DATE	ACCOUNT TITLES AND EXPLANATION	P.R.	DEBIT	CREDIT

Problem VI

Riverview Properties operates an apartment building. On December 31, at the end of an annual accounting period, its Rent Earned account had a $335,500 credit balance, and the Unearned Rent account had a $3,600 credit balance. The following information was available for the year-end adjustments: (a) the credit balance in the Unearned Rent account resulted from a tenant paying his rent for six months in advance beginning on November 1; (b) also, a tenant in temporary financial difficulties had not paid his rent for the month of December. The amount due was $475.

Required: Enter the necessary adjustments directly in the T-accounts below.

Rent Receivable	Unearned Rent	Rent Earned
	Nov. 1 3,600	Balance 335,500

After the foregoing adjustments are entered in the accounts, the company's Rent Earned account has a $_____ balance which should appear on its income statement as revenue earned during the year. Its Unearned Rent account has a $_____ balance, and this should appear on the company's balance sheet as a _____. Likewise, the company's Rent Receivable account has a $_____ balance, and this should appear on its balance sheet as a _____.

Problem VII

Under the cash basis of accounting, revenues are reported as being earned in the accounting period in which _____; expenses are charged to the period in which _____; and net income for the period is the difference between _____ and _____. Under the accrual basis of accounting, revenues are credited to the period in which _____, expenses are _____ with revenues, and no consideration is given as to when cash is received or disbursed.

Problem VIII (This problem applies to Appendix A.)

The following statements are either true or false. Place a (T) in the parentheses before each true statement and an (F) before each false statement.

1.   (   ) If a business follows the practice of debiting prepayments of expenses to expense accounts, the adjusting entries for prepaid expenses require debits to prepaid expense accounts.

2.   (   ) If a business records receipts of unearned revenues with debits to cash and credits to revenue accounts, no adjusting entries are required at the end of the period.

Problem IX (This problem applies to Appendix A.)

You are given several words, phrases, or numbers to choose from in completing each of the following statements or in answering the following questions. In each case select the one that best completes the statement or answers the question and place its letter in the answer space provided.

_____ 1. Richley Company prepares monthly financial statements and follows the procedure of crediting revenue accounts when it records cash receipts of unearned revenues. During April, the business received $4,800 for services to be rendered during April and May. On April 30, $2,000 of the amounts received had been earned. What is the adjusting journal entry on April 30 for service fees?

    a. Service Fees Earned 2,000

         Unearned Service Fees.. 2,000

    b. Unearned Service Fees 2,800

         Service Fees Earned 2,800

    c. Cash..2,000

         Service Fees Earned 2,000

    d. Unearned Service Fees 2,000

         Service Fees Earned 2,000

    e. Service Fees Earned 2,800

         Unearned Service Fees... 2,800

_____ 2. Xu Company prepares monthly financial statements. On August 31, the balance in the Office Supplies account was $300. During September, $500 of supplies were purchased and debited to Office Supplies Expense. What is the adjusting journal entry on September 30 to adjust for the supplies assuming a September inventory of supplies showed that $250 were on hand.

    a. Office Supplies..350

         Office Supplies Expense.. 350

    b. Office Supplies Expense 250

         Office Supplies.. 250

    c. Office Supplies Expense 50

         Office Supplies.. 50

    d. Office Supplies Expense...350

         Office Supplies.. 350

    e. Office Supplies...250

         Office Supplies Expense 250

Solutions for Chapter 4

Problem I

1. T
2. F
3. T
4. T
5. F

Problem II

1. D
2. C
3. C
4. E
5. D
6. C

Problem III

Problem IV

Oct. 31	Rent Expense		515.00	
	Prepaid Rent			515.00
31	Office Supplies Expense		35.00	
	Office Supplies			35.00
31	Amortization Expense, Office Equipment		35.00	
	Accumulated Depr., Office Equipment			35.00

Cash			
Date	Debit	Credit	Balance
Oct 1	4,000.00		4,000.00
1		1,545.00	2,455.00
1		925.00	1,530.00
31	1,800.00		3,330.00
31		800.00	2,530.00

Accounts Payable			
Date	Debit	Credit	Balance
Oct. 2		775.00	775.00

Office Supplies			
Oct. 2	75.00		75.00
31		35.00	40.00

George Lee, Capital			
Oct. 1		4,000.00	4,000.00

George Lee, Withdrawals			
Oct. 31	800.00		800.00

Prepaid Rent			
Oct. 1	1,545.00		1,545.00
31		515.00	1,030.00

Repair Services Revenue			
Oct. 31		1,800.00	1,800.00

Amort. Expense, Office Equipment			
Oct. 31	35.00		35.00

Office Equipment			
Oct. 1	925.00		925.00
2	700.00		1,625.00

Rent Expense			
Oct. 31	515.00		515.00

Accumulated Amort., Office Equipment			
Oct. 31		35.00	35.00

Office Supplies Expense			
Oct. 31	35.00		35.00

GEORGE LEE
Adjusted Trial Balance
October 31, 2001

Cash	$2,530.00	
Office Supplies	40.00	
Prepaid rent	1,030.00	
Office equipment	1,625.00	
Accumulated amortization, office equipment		$ 35.00
Accounts payable		775.00
George Lee, capital		4,000.00
George Lee, withdrawals	800.00	
Repair services revenue		1,800.00
Amortization expense, office equipment	35.00	
Rent expense	515.00	
Office supplies expense	35.00	
Totals	$6,610.00	$6,610.00

GEORGE LEE
Income Statement
For Month Ended October 31, 2001

Revenue:		
Repair services revenue		$1,800.00
Operating expenses:		
Amortization expense, office equipment	$ 35.00	
Rent expense	515.00	
Office supplies expense	35.00	
Total operating expenses		585.00
Net income		$1,215.00

GEORGE LEE
Statement of Owner's Equity
For Month Ended October 31, 2001

George Lee, capital, October 1, 2001		$4,000.00
October net income	$1,215.00	
Less withdrawals	800.00	
Excess of income over withdrawals		415.00
George Lee, capital, October 31, 2001		$4,415.00

GEORGE LEE
Balance Sheet
October 31, 2001
Assets

Cash		$2,530.00
Office supplies		40.00
Prepaid rent		1,030.00
Office equipment	$1,625.00	
Less accumulated amortization	35.00	1,590.00
Total assets		$5,190.00

Liabilities

Accounts payable		$775.00

Owner's Equity

George Lee, Capital, October 31, 2001		4,415.00
Total liabilities and owner's equity		$5,190.00

Problem V

a.

	Cash				Wages Expense	
	Oct. 5	400.00		Oct. 5	400.00	
	12	400.00		12	400.00	
	19	400.00		19	400.00	
	26	400.00		26	400.00	
				31	240.00	

	Wages Payable	
	Oct. 31	240.00

b. $1,840.00; $240.00; accrued

c. Nov 2 Salaries Expense.. 160.00
            Salaries Payable 240.00
            Cash...   400.00

Problem VI

	Rent Receivable				Unearned Rent		
Dec. 31	475			Dec. 31	1,200	Nov. 1	3,600

	Rent Earned	
	Bal.	335,500
	Dec. 31	1,200
	31	475

Rent Earned, $337,175
Unearned Rent, $2,400, liability
Rent Receivable, $475, asset

Problem VII

they are received in cash, they are paid, revenue receipts, expense disbursements, earned, matched

Problem VIII

1. T
2. F

Problem IX

1. E
2. C

CHAPTER 5
COMPLETING THE ACCOUNTING CYCLE
AND CLASSIFYING ACCOUNTS

Learning Objective 1:

Prepare a work sheet and explain its usefulness.

Summary

A work sheet can be a useful tool in preparing and analyzing financial statements. It is helpful at the end of a period in preparing adjusting entries, an adjusted trial balance, and financial statements. A work sheet often contains five pairs of columns for an unadjusted trial balance, the adjustments, an adjusted trial balance, an income statement, and the balance sheet (including the statement of owner's equity).

Learning Objective 2:

Describe the closing process.

Summary

The closing process is the final step of the accounting cycle that prepares accounts for recording the transactions of the next period.

Learning Objective 3:

Explain why temporary accounts are closed each period.

Summary

Temporary accounts are closed at the end of each accounting period for two main reasons. First, the closing process updates the owner's capital account to include the effects of all revenue, expense, and withdrawals transactions and events recorded for the period. Second, it prepares revenue, expense and withdrawals accounts for the next reporting period by giving them zero balances.

Learning Objective 4:

Describe and prepare closing entries.

Summary

Recording and posting closing entries transfers the end-of-period balances in revenue, expense and withdrawals accounts to the owner's capital account. Closing entries involves four steps: (1) close credit balances in revenue accounts to income summary, (2) close debit balances in expense accounts to income summary, (3) close income summary to owner's capital, and (4) close withdrawals account to owner's capital.

Learning Objective 5:

Explain and prepare a post-closing trial balance.

Summary

A post-closing trial balance is a list of permanent accounts and their balances after all closing entries are journalized and posted. Permanent accounts are asset, liability and owner's equity accounts. The purpose of a post-closing trial balance is to verify that (1) total debits equal total credits for permanent accounts and (2) all temporary accounts have zero balances.

Learning Objective 6:

Review steps in the accounting cycle.

Summary

The accounting cycle consists of nine steps: (1) analyze transactions, (2) journalize, (3) posting, (4) an unadjusted trial balance, (5) adjusting, (6) an adjusted trial balance, (7) statement preparation, (8) closing, (9) a post-closing trial balance. If a work sheet is prepared, it covers steps 4–6. Reversing entries is also an optional step that is done between steps 9 and 1.

Learning Objective 7:

Explain and prepare a classified balance sheet.

Summary

Classified balance sheets usually report four groups of assets: current assets, long-term investments, plant and equipment, and intangible assets. Also, they include at least two groups of liabilities: current and long-term. Owner's equity for proprietorships reports the capital account balance.

Learning Objective 8 (Appendix 5A):

Prepare reversing entries and explain their purpose.

Summary

Reversing entries are an optional step. They are applied to accrued assets and liabilities. The purpose of reversing entries is to simplify subsequent journal entries. Financial statements are unaffected by the choice to use or not use reversing entries.

Chapter Outline

I. **Work Sheet as a Tool**—Useful to organize accounting information. (Not a financial statement) The informal documents are called *working papers*.

  A. Benefits include: useful in preparing interim financial statements, captures linked accounting information, helps organize an audit, helps avoid errors.

  B. Steps to prepare a work sheet with five sets of double columns:

    1. Enter unadjusted trial balance in the first two columns.

    2. Enter adjustments in the third and fourth columns. Total columns to verify debit adjustments equal credit adjustments.

    3. Prepare adjusted trial balance by combining the adjustments with the unadjusted balances for each account. Total Adjusted Trial Balance columns to verify debits equal credits.

    4. Extend adjusted trial balance amounts to financial statement columns.

    5. Enter net income (or loss) and balance the financial statement columns.

    6. Prepare financial statements from work sheet information.

II. **Closing Process**—an important step to prepare accounts for recording the transactions of the next period.

  A. In the closing process we must:

    1. Identify accounts for closing.

    2. Record and post closing entries.

    3. Prepare a post-closing trial balance.

  B. Closing entries are a necessary step to ensure that:

    1. Revenue, expense, and withdrawals accounts (a) are reflected in the owner's equity and (b) begin with zero balances to measure the results from the period just ending.

    2. Owner's capital account reflects (a) increases from net income and (b) decreases from net losses and withdrawals from the period just ending.

  C. Temporary and Permanent Accounts

    1. Temporary (or nominal) accounts accumulate data related to one accounting period. (All income statement accounts, withdrawals accounts, and the Income Summary.)

    2. Permanent (or real) accounts report on activities related to one or more future accounting periods. They carry their ending balances into the next period. (All balance sheet accounts.)

    3. The closing process applies only to temporary accounts.

    D. Recording and Posting Closing Entries

        1. Transfer balances of temporary accounts using a new temporary account called Income Summary. The four closing entries are:

            a. Close credit balances in revenue accounts to Income Summary.

            b. Close debit balances in expense accounts to Income Summary.

            c. Close Income Summary to Owner's Capital.

            Note: Income Summary, prior to closing, will have a credit balance equal to net income or a debit balance equal to net loss. Therefore this entry will credit capital for the net income or debit capital for a net loss.

            d. Close Withdrawals account to Owner's Capital account.

    E. Post-Closing Trial Balance

        1. Prepared after all closing entries are journalized and posted.

        2. Verifies that total debits equal total credits for permanent accounts, and all temporary accounts have zero balances.

III.   **Reviewing the Accounting Cycle**—the sequence of accounting procedures followed each accounting period:

    A. Analyze transactions

    B. Journalize

    C. Posting

    D. Unadjusted trial balance

    E. Adjusting

    F. Adjusted trial balance

    G. Statement preparation

    H. Closing

    I. Post-closing trial balance

IV. **Classified Balance Sheet**—organizes assets and liabilities into sub-groups:

    A. Current assets—cash and other resources that are expected to be sold, collected, or used within the longer of one year or the company's operating cycle; cash, temporary investments in marketable securities, accounts receivable, notes receivable, merchandise inventory, prepaid expenses.

    B. Long-term investments—held for more than one year or the operating cycle; often includes land held for future expansion.

    C. Capital assets:

        1. Plant and equipment—tangible long-lived assets used to produce or sell products and services; equipment, vehicles, buildings, land.

        2. Intangible assets—Long-term resources used to produce or sell products and services; do not have a physical form; their value comes from the privileges or rights granted to or held by the owner; goodwill.

    D. Current liabilities—obligations due to be paid or settled, usually out of current assets, within one year or the operating cycle; accounts payable, notes payable, wages payable, taxes payable, interest payable, unearned revenues.

    E. Long-term liabilities—obligations that are not due within one year or the operating cycle of the business; notes payable, mortgages payable, bonds payable, lease obligations.

    F. Owner's equity—the owner's claim on the assets of a company. Reported in the equity section as owner's capital for a proprietorship, partner's capital for a partnership, and shareholders' equity for a corporation.

V. **Appendix 5A: Reversing Entries and Account Numbering**

    A. Reversing entries are optional entries prepared after closing entries and dated the first day of the new period.

    B. Reversing entries are usually applied to asset and liability account balances that arose from the accrual of revenues and expenses.

    C. The accrued asset and liability account balances are transferred to related revenue and expense accounts.

    D. When reversing entries are used, subsequent cash receipts (and payments) are recorded in revenue (and expense) accounts.

THE ACCOUNTING CYCLE
This Cycle Assumes a Work Sheet is Used

STEPS	PURPOSE	TIMING
1. Analyze transaction	In preparation for journalizing	During the period
2. Journalize	Record debits and credits in a journal	During the period
3. Posting	Transfer debits and credits from journal entries to the ledger accounts	During the period
4. Work sheet	• Unadjusted trial balance columns: summarize ledger accounts and amounts	End of period
	• Adjusting columns: record adjustments to bring account balances up to date; journalize and post adjusting entries to the accounts	
	• Adjusted trial balance columns: Summarize adjusted ledger accounts and amounts	
5. Statement preparation	Use adjusted trial balance to prepare statements	End of period
6. Closing	Journalize and post entries to close temporary accounts and update the owner's capital account.	End of period
7. Post-closing trial balance	Test clerical accuracy of adjusting and closing steps.	End of period

MUSIC COMPONENTS
BALANCE SHEET
JANUARY 31, 2001

Assets

Current assets:

Cash	$ 6,500	
Temporary investments	2,100	
Accounts receivable	4,400	
Notes receivable	1,500	
Merchandise inventory	27,500	
Prepaid expenses	2,400	
Total current assets		$ 44,400

Long-term investments:

CanCom common shares	18,000	
Land held for future expansion	48,000	
Total investments		66,000

Capital assets:

Plant and equipment:			
Store equipment	$ 33,200		
Less: Accumulated amortization	8,000	25,200	
Buildings	$170,000		
Less Accumulated Amortization	45,000	125,000	
Land		73 200	
Total plant and equipment			223,400
Intangible assets:			
Trademark			10,000
Total Assets			$343,800

Liabilities

Current liabilities:

Accounts Payable	$ 15,300	
Wages Payable	3,200	
Notes Payable	3,000	
Current portion of long-term liabilities	7,500	
Total current liabilities		$ 29,000

Long-term liabilities:

Notes payable (less current portion)	150,000	
Total liabilities		$179,000

Owner's equity

Donald Bowie, capital		164,800
Total liabilities and owner's equity		$343,800

Problem I

The following statements are either true or false. Place a (T) in the parentheses before each true statement and an (F) before each false statement.

1. (   ) Throughout the current period, one could refer to the balance of the Income Summary account to determine the amount of net income or loss that was earned in the prior accounting period.

2. (   ) The only reason why the Statement of Owner's Equity or Balance Sheet columns of a work sheet might be out of balance would be if an error had been made in sorting revenue and expense data from the Adjusted Trial Balance columns of the work sheet.

3. (   ) If the Income Statement columns of a work sheet are equal after transferring from the Adjusted Trial Balance columns, then it can be concluded that there is no net income (or loss).

4. (   ) On a work sheet, net income would be overstated if a liability was extended into the Income Statement—Credit column.

5. (   ) After all closing entries are posted at the end of an accounting period, the Income Summary account balance is zero.

Problem II

You are given several words, phrases, or numbers to choose from in completing each of the following statements or in answering the following question. In each case select the one that best completes the statement or answers the question and place its letter in the answer space provided.

_____ 1. Inventory, Rent Expense, and The Owner, Capital would be sorted to which respective columns in completing a work sheet?

   a. Statement of Owner's Equity or Balance Sheet—Debit; Income Statement—Debit; and Statement of Owner's Equity or Balance Sheet—Debit.

   b. Statement of Owner's Equity or Balance Sheet—Debit; Income Statement—Debit; and Statement of Owner's Equity or Balance Sheet—Credit.

   c. Statement of Owner's Equity or Balance Sheet—Debit; Income Statement— Credit; and Statement of Owner's Equity or Balance Sheet—Debit.

   d. Statement of Owner's Equity or Balance Sheet—Debit; Income Statement— Credit; and Statement of Owner's Equity or Balance Sheet—Credit.

   e. Statement of Owner's Equity or Balance Sheet—Credit; Income Statement— Credit; and Statement of Owner's Equity or Balance Sheet—Credit.

2. Based on the following T-accounts and their end-of-period balances, what will be the balance of the Bill Atkins, Capital account after the closing entries are posted?

Bill Atkins, Capital			Bill Atkins, Withdrawals			Income Summary	
	Dec. 31	7,000	Dec. 31	9,600			

Revenue			Rent Expense			Salaries Expense	
	Dec. 31	29,700	Dec. 31	3,600		Dec. 31	7,200

Insurance Expense			Amort. Expense, Equipment			Accum. Amort. Equipment	
Dec. 31	920		Dec. 31	500			Dec.31	500

a. $12,880 Debit.
b. $12,880 Credit.
c. $24,480 Credit.
d. $14,880 Credit.
e. $10,480 Debit.

3. The following items appeared on a December 31 work sheet. Based on the following information, what are the totals in the Statement of Owner's Equity or Balance Sheet columns?

	Unadjusted Trial Balance		Adjustments	
	Debit	Credit	Debit	Credit
Cash	975			
Supplies	180			70
Prepaid insurance	3,600			150
Equipment	10,320			
Accounts payable		1,140		
Unearned fees		4,500	375	
The Owner, capital		9,180		
The Owner, withdrawals	1,650			
Fees earned		5,850		375
				300
Salaries expense	2,100		315	
Rent expense	1,500			
Utilities expense	345			
	20,670	20,670		
Insurance expense			150	
Supplies expense			70	
Amortization expense, equipment			190	
Accumulated amortization, equipment				190
Salaries payable				315
Accounts receivable			300	
			1,400	1,400

a. $16,805.
b. $16,505.
c. $14,950.
d. $14,820.
e. Some other amount.

_____ 4. In what order are the following steps in the accounting cycle performed?
1) Unadjusted trial balance
2) Closing entries
3) Journalize
4) Post-closing trial balance
5) Financial statement preparation
6) Analyze transactions
7) Adjusting entries
8) Posting
9) Adjusted trial balance
   a. (3), (6), (7), (8), (1), (9), (5), (2), (4)
   b. (6), (3), (8), (1), (7), (9), (5), (2), (4)
   c. (3), (1), (7), (6), (8), (5), (9), (4), (2)
   d. (6), (7), (8), (1), (3), (5), (9), (4), (2)
   e. (6), (3), (1), (8), (9), (5), (7), (2), (4)

_____ 5. Temporary accounts are:

   a. Accounts that are not closed at the end of the accounting period; therefore, assets, liabilities and equity accounts.

   b. Accounts used to record the owner's investment in the business plus any more or less permanent changes in the owner's equity.

   c. Accounts the balance of which is subtracted from the balance of an associated account to show a more proper amount for the item recorded in the associated account.

   d. Also called nominal accounts.

   e. Also called real accounts.

_____ 6. The following information is available from the financial statements of California Company:

Current assets	$ 195,000
Current liabilities	113,500
Total liabilities	441,500
Shareholder's Equity	408,500

The amount of capital assets showing on the balance sheet is:
   a. $328,000
   b. $308,500
   c. $246,500
   d. $441,500
   e. $655,000

Problem III

Many of the important ideas and concepts discussed in Chapter 5 are reflected in the following list of key terms. Test your understanding of these terms by matching the appropriate definitions with the terms. Record the number identifying the most appropriate definition in the blank space next to each term.

_____ Classified balance sheet
_____ Closing entries
_____ Closing process
_____ Current assets
_____ Current liabilities
_____ Income summary
_____ Intangible assets
_____ Long-term investments
_____ Long-term liabilities
_____ Nominal accounts
_____ Operating cycle of a business

_____ Owner's equity
_____ Permanent accounts
_____ Plant and equipment
_____ Post-closing trial balance
_____ Pro forma statements
_____ Real accounts
_____ Reversing entries
_____ Temporary accounts
_____ Unclassified balance sheet
_____ Work sheet
_____ Working papers

1. Another name for permanent accounts.

2. Assets such as notes receivable or investments in shares and bonds that are held for more than one year or the operating cycle.

3. A balance sheet that broadly groups the assets, liabilities and owner's equity.

4. Journal entries recorded at the end of each accounting period that transfer the end-of-period balances in revenues, expense, and withdrawals accounts to the permanent owner's capital account in order to prepare for the upcoming period and update the owner's capital account for the events of the period just finished.

5. Also called plant assets; are tangible long-lived assets used to produce or sell products and services.

6. A temporary account used only in the closing process to where the balances of revenue and expense accounts are transferred; its balance equals net income or net loss and is transferred to the owner's capital account.

7. The average time between paying cash for employee salaries or merchandise and receiving cash from customers.

8. Accounts that are used to report on activities related to one or more future accounting periods; their balances are carried into the next period, and include all balance sheets accounts; permanent account balances are not closed as long as the company continues to own the asses, owe the liabilities, and have owner's equity; also called real accounts.

9. Optional entries recorded at the beginning of a new period that prepare the accounts for simplified journal entries subsequent to accrual adjusting entries.

10. Cash or other assets that are expected to be sold, collected, or used within the longer of one year or the company's operating cycle.

11. A balance sheet that presents the assets and liabilities in relevant subgroups.

12. Statements that show the effects of the proposed transactions as if the transactions had already occurred.

13. Long-term assets (resources) used to produce or sell products or services; these assets lack physical form.

14. A 10-column spreadsheet used to draft a company's unadjusted trial balance, adjusting entries, adjusted trial balance, and financial statements; an optional step in the accounting process.

15. Obligations due to be paid or settled within the longer of one year or the operating cycle.

16. Accounts that are used to describe revenues, expenses, and owner's withdrawals for one accounting period; they are closed at the end of the reporting period.

17. Obligations that are not due to be paid within the longer of one year or the operating cycle.

18. A step at the end of the accounting period that prepares accounts for recording the transactions of the next period.

19. A list of permanent accounts and their balances from the ledger after all closing entries are journalized and posted; a list of balances for all accounts not closed.

20. The owner's claim on the assets of a company.

21. Internal documents that are used to assist the preparers in doing the analyses and organizing the information for reports to be presented to internal and external decision makers.

22. Another name for temporary accounts.

Problem IV

Complete the following by filling in the blanks.

1. A work sheet is prepared after all transactions are recorded but before _____
_____.

2. Revenue accounts have credit balances; consequently, to close a revenue account and make it show a zero balance, the revenue account is _____ and the Income Summary account is _____ for the amount of the balance.

3. In extending the amounts in the Adjusted Trial Balance columns of a work sheet to the proper Income Statement or Statement of Changes in Owner's Equity and Balance Sheet columns, two decisions are:
   (a)_____and
   (b)_____.

4. Expense accounts have debit balances; therefore, expense accounts are_____ and the Income Summary account is _____ in closing the expense accounts.

5. In preparing a work sheet for a business, its unadjusted account balances are entered in the _____ of the work sheet form, after which the _____ are entered in the second pair of columns. Next, the unadjusted trial balance amounts and the amounts in the Adjustments columns are combined to secure an _____ in the third pair of columns.

6. Only balance sheet accounts should have balances appearing on the post-closing trial balance because the balances of all temporary accounts are reduced to _____ in the closing procedure.

7. Closing entries are necessary because if at the end of an accounting period the revenue and expense accounts are to show only one period's revenues and expenses, they must begin the period with _____ balances, and closing entries cause the revenue and expense accounts to begin a new period with _____ balances.

8. Closing entries accomplish two purposes: (1) they cause all _____ accounts to begin the new accounting period with zero balances, and (2) they transfer the net effect of the past period's _____, _____, and withdrawal transactions to the owner's capital account.

Problem V

The unfinished year-end work sheet of Jason's Home Shop appears on the next page.

Required:

1. Complete the work sheet using the following adjustments information:

    a. A $725 inventory of shop supplies indicates that $1,037 of shop supplies have been used during the year.

    b. Amortization of shop equipment was $475 during the year.

    c. On December 31, wages of $388 have been earned by the one employee but are unpaid because payment is not due.

2. After completing the work sheet, prepare the year-end adjusting and closing entries.

3. Post the adjusting and closing entries to the accounts that are provided in the abbreviated general ledger.

4. After posting the adjusting and closing entries, prepare a post-closing trial balance.

JASON'S HOME SHOP
Work Sheet For the Year Ended December 31, 2001

ACCOUNT	UNADJUSTED TRIAL BALANCE DR.	UNADJUSTED TRIAL BALANCE CR.	ADJUSTMENTS DR.	ADJUSTMENTS CR.	ADJUSTED TRIAL BALANCE DR.	ADJUSTED TRIAL BALANCE CR.	INCOME STATEMENT DR.	INCOME STATEMENT CR.	STMT. OF O.E. AND BALANCE SHEET DR.	STMT. OF O.E. AND BALANCE SHEET CR.
Cash	2 8 7 5 00									
Accounts receivable	2 0 0 0 00									
Shop supplies	1 7 6 2 00									
Shop equipment	5 1 2 5 00									
Accumulated amortization, shop equipment		7 2 5 00								
Accounts payable		5 7 5 00								
Jason Painter, capital		5 5 0 0 00								
Jason Painter, Withdrawals	30 0 0 0 00									
Repair services Revenue		55 7 8 5 00								
Wages expense	18 2 5 0 00									
Rent expense	2 5 0 0 00									
Miscellaneous Expenses	7 3 00									
	62 5 8 5 00	62 5 8 5 00								
Shop supplies Expense										
Amortization expense, shop Equipment										
Wages payable										

DATE	ACCOUNT TITLES AND EXPLANATION	P.R.	DEBIT	CREDIT

GENERAL LEDGER

Cash

Date	Debit	Credit	Balance
Dec. 31			2,875.00

Accounts Receivable

Date	Debit	Credit	Balance
Dec. 31			2,000.00

Shop Supplies

Date	Debit	Credit	Balance
Dec. 31			1,762.00

Shop Equipment

Date	Debit	Credit	Balance
Dec. 31			5,125.00

Accum. Amort., Shop Equipment

Date	Debit	Credit	Balance
Dec. 31			725.00

Accounts Payable

Date	Debit	Credit	Balance
Dec. 31			575.00

Wages Payable

Date	Debit	Credit	Balance

Jason Painter, Capital

Date	Debit	Credit	Balance
Dec. 31			5,500.00

Jason Painter, Withdrawals

Date	Debit	Credit	Balance
Dec. 31			30,000.00

Repair Services Revenue

Date	Debit	Credit	Balance
Dec. 31			55,785.00

Amort. Expense, Shop Equipment

Date	Debit	Credit	Balance

Wages Expense

Date	Debit	Credit	Balance
Dec. 31			18,250.00

Rent Expense

Date	Debit	Credit	Balance
Dec. 31			2,500.00

Shop Supplies Expense

Date	Debit	Credit	Balance

Miscellaneous Expenses

Date	Debit	Credit	Balance
Dec. 31			73.00

Income Summary

Date	Debit	Credit	Balance

JASON'S HOME SHOP

Post-Closing Trial Balance

December 31, 2001

Cash							
Accounts receivable							
Shop supplies							
Shop equipment							
Accumulated amortization, shop equipment							
Accounts payable							
Wages payable							
Jason Painter, capital							
Totals							

Problem VI

Based on the following end-of-period information, prepare closing entries assuming that adjusting entries have been properly recorded.

1. Revenues, $285,000.

2. Expenses, $250,000.

3. Your name, capital, beginning balance, $110,000.

4. Your name, withdrawals, $30,000.

GENERAL JOURNAL

Page 1

DATE	ACCOUNT TITLES AND EXPLANATION	P.R.	DEBIT	CREDIT

5. Calculate the ending balance in the owner's capital account.

Your name, capital

Problem VII (This problem applies to Appendix 5A.)

The following statements are either true or false. Place a (T) in the parentheses before each true statement and an (F) before each false statement.

1. ( ) After the adjusting, closing, and reversing entries are posted to an account where there were end of-period adjustments of accrued items, the account will have an opposite from normal balance.

2. ( ) Some companies initially record prepaid expenses with debits to expense accounts and then make end-of-period adjusting entries to transfer unexpired amounts to asset accounts. These companies may then use reversing entries to transfer the unexpired amounts back into expense accounts.

Problem VIII (This problem applies to Appendix 5A.)

You are given several words, phrases, or numbers to choose from in completing each of the following statements or in answering the following questions. In each case select the one that best completes the statement or answers the question and place its letter in the answer space provided.

_____ 1. The December 31,2001, adjusting entries for Mary Loretti's interior design company included accrual of $760 in assistant salaries. This amount will be paid on January 10, as part of the normal $1,200 salary for two weeks. The bookkeeper for the company uses reversing entries where appropriate. The entry to record the payment of the assistant's salary January 10,2002, was:

Jan. 10 Salaries Expense	1,200	
Cash		1,200

What was the January 1, 2002, reversing entry?

a.	Salaries Payable	760	
	Salaries Expense	440	
	Cash		1,200
b.	Salaries Payable	440	
	Salaries Expense		440
c.	Salaries Payable	760	
	Salaries Expense		760
d.	Cash	1,200	
	Salaries Expense		1,200

e. The bookkeeper would not make a reversing entry for this transaction.

_____ 2. On December 31, 2001, K Company accrued salaries expense with an adjusting entry. No reversing entry was made and the payment of the salaries during January 2002 was correctly recorded. If X Company had recorded an entry on January 1, 2002, to reverse the accrual, and the subsequent payment was correctly recorded, the effect on the 2002 financial statements of using the reversing entry would have been:

a. to increase net income and reduce liabilities.

b. to increase 2002 expense and reduce assets.

c. to decrease 2002 expense and increase liabilities.

d. to decrease 2002 expense and decrease liabilities.

e. No effect.

Solutions for Chapter 5

Problem I

1. F
2. F
3. T
4. T
5. T

Problem II

1. B
2. D
3. A
4. B
5. D
6. E

Problem III

Problem IV

1. the adjustments are entered in the accounts

2. debited, credited

3. (a) Is the item a debit or a credit?

   (b) On which statement does it appear?

4. credited, debited

5. Unadjusted Trial Balance columns; adjustments; adjusted trial balance

6. zero

7. zero, zero

8. temporary or nominal, revenue, expense

Problem V

JASON'S HOME SHOP
Work Sheet for Year Ended December 31, 2001

	Unadjusted Trial Balance Dr.	Unadjusted Trial Balance Cr.	Adjustments Dr.	Adjustments Cr.	Adjusted Trial Balance Dr.	Adjusted Trial Balance Cr.	Income Statement Dr.	Income Statement Cr.	Statement of O.E. and Balance Sheet Dr.	Statement of O.E. and Balance Sheet Cr.
Cash	2,875				2,875				2,875	
Accounts receivable	2,000				2,000				2,000	
Shop supplies	1,762			(a)1,037	725				725	
Shop equipment	5,125				5,125				5,125	
Accum. amort., shop equipment		725		(b) 475		1,200				1,200
Accounts payable		575				575				575
Jason Painter, capital		5,500				5,500				5,500
Jason Painter, withdrawals	30,000				30,000				30,000	
Repair services revenue		55,785				55,785		55,785		
Wages expense	18,250			(c)388	18,638		18,638			
Rent expense	2,500				2,500		2,500			
Miscellaneous expenses	73				73		73			
	62,585	62,585								
Shop supplies expense			(a)1037		1,037		1,037			
Amortization expense, shop equipment			(b) 475		475		475			
Wages payable				(c) 388		388				388
			1,900	1,900	63,448	63,448	22,723	55,785	40,725	7,663
Net income							33,062			33,062
							55,785	55,785	40,725	40,725

Dec. 31 Shop Supplies Expense 1,037
       Shop Supplies 1,037

31 Amort. Expense, Shop Equipment ... 475
       Accumulated Amort., Shop Equipment ... 475

31 Wages Expense 388
       Wages Payable 388

31 Repair Services Revenue 55,785
       Income Summary 55,785

31 Income Summary 22,723
       Rent Expense 2,500
       Wages Expense 18,638
       Miscellaneous Expenses 73
       Shop Supplies Expense 1,037
       Amort. Expense, Shop Equipment 475

31 Income Summary 33,062
       Jason Painter, Capital 33,062

31 Jason Painter, Capital 30,000
       Jason Painter, Withdrawals 30,000

GENERAL LEDGER

Cash

Date	Debit	Credit	Balance
Dec. 31			2,875.00

Accounts Receivable

Date	Debit	Credit	Balance
Dec. 31			2,000.00

Shop Supplies

Date	Debit	Credit	Balance
Dec. 31			1,762.00
31		1,037.00	725.00

Shop Equipment

Date	Debit	Credit	Balance
Dec. 31			5,125.00

Accum. Amort., Shop Equipment

Date	Debit	Credit	Balance
Dec. 31			725.00
31		475.00	1,200.00

Accounts Payable

Date	Debit	Credit	Balance
Dec. 31			575.00

Wages Payable

Date	Debit	Credit	Balance
Dec. 31		388.00	388.00

Jason Painter, Capital

Date	Debit	Credit	Balance
Dec. 31			5,500.00
31		33,062.00	38,562.00
31	30,000.00		8,562.00

Jason Painter, Withdrawals

Date	Debit	Credit	Balance
Dec. 31			30,000.00
31		30,000.00	-0-

Repair Services Revenue

Date	Debit	Credit	Balance
Dec. 31			55,785.00
31	55,785.00		-0-

Amort. Expense, Shop Equipment

Date	Debit	Credit	Balance
Dec. 31	475.00		475.00
31		475.00	-0-

Wages Expense

Date	Debit	Credit	Balance
Dec. 31			18,250.00
31	388.00		18,638.00
31		18,638.00	-0-

Rent Expense

Date	Debit	Credit	Balance
Dec. 31			2,500.00
31		2,500.00	-0-

Shop Supplies Expense

Date	Debit	Credit	Balance
Dec. 31	1,037.00		1,037.00
31		1,037.00	-0-

Miscellaneous Expenses

Date	Debit	Credit	Balance
Dec. 31			73.00
31		73.00	-0-

Income Summary

Date	Debit	Credit	Balance
Dec. 31		55,785.00	55,785.00
31	22,723.00		33,062.00
31	33,062.00		-0-

JASON'S HOME SHOP

Post-Closing Trial Balance

December 31, 2001

Cash	$2,875	
Accounts receivable	2,000	
Shop supplies...	725	
Shop equipment	5,125	
Accumulated amortization, shop equipment		$1,200
Accounts payable..		575
Wages payable..		388
Jason Painter, capital		8,562
	$10,725	$10,725

Problem VI

GENERAL JOURNAL

Page 1

DATE		ACCOUNT TITLES AND EXPLANATION	P.R.	DEBIT						CREDIT					
Dec	31	Revenues		28	5	0	0	0	00						
		Income summary								28	5	0	0	0	00
Dec	31	Income summary		25	0	0	0	0	00						
		Expenses								25	0	0	0	0	00
Dec	31	Income summary		3	5	0	0	0	00						
		Your name, capital								3	5	0	0	0	00
Dec	31	Your name, capital		3	0	0	0	0	00						
		Your name, withdrawals								3	0	0	0	0	00

1. Calculate the ending balance in the owner's capital account.

Your name, capital

		$110,000	Beginning balance
		35,000	Net income
Withdrawals	$ 30,000		
		$115,000	Ending balance

Problem VII

1. T

2. T

Problem VIII

1. C

2. E

CHAPTER 6
ACCOUNTING FOR MERCHANDISING ACTIVITIES

Learning Objective 1:

Describe merchandising activities and identify business examples.

Summary

Operations of merchandising companies involve buying products and reselling them.

Learning Objective 2:

Identify and explain the important components of income for a merchandising company.

Summary

A merchandiser's costs on an income statement include an amount for cost of goods sold. Gross profit, or gross margin, equals net sales minus cost of goods sold.

Learning Objective 3:

Identify and explain the inventory asset of a merchandising company.

Summary

The current asset section of a merchandising company's balance sheet includes merchandise inventory. Merchandise inventory refers to the products a merchandiser sells and are on hand at the balance sheet date.

Learning Objective 4:

Describe both periodic and perpetual inventory systems.

Summary

A perpetual inventory system continuously tracks the cost of goods on hand and the cost of goods sold. A periodic system accumulates the cost of goods purchased during the period and does not compute the amount of inventory on hand or the cost of goods sold until the end of a period.

Learning Objective 5:

Analyze and record transactions for merchandise purchases using a perpetual system.

Summary

For a perpetual inventory system, purchases net of trade discounts are added (debited) to the Merchandise Inventory account. Purchase discounts and purchase returns and allowances are subtracted (credited) to Merchandise Inventory, and transportation-in costs are added (debited) to Merchandise Inventory. Many companies keep supplementary records to accumulate information about the total amounts of purchases, purchase discounts, purchase returns and allowances, and transportation-in.

Learning Objective 6:

Analyze and record transactions for sales of merchandise using a perpetual system.

Summary

A merchandiser records sales at list price less any trade discounts. The cost of items sold is transferred from Merchandise Inventory to Cost of Goods Sold. Refunds or credits given to customers for unsatisfactory merchandise are recorded (debited) in Sales Returns and Allowances, a contra account to Sales. If merchandise is returned and restored to inventory, the cost of this merchandise is removed from Cost of Goods Sold and transferred back to Merchandise Inventory. When cash discounts from the sales price are offered and customers pay within the discount period, the seller records (debits) discounts in Sales Discounts, a contra account to Sales. Debit and credit memoranda are documents sent between buyers and sellers to communicate that the sender is either debiting or crediting an account of the recipient.

Learning Objective 7:

Prepare adjustments for a merchandising company.

Summary

With a perpetual inventory system, it is often required to make an adjustment for inventory shrinkage. This is computed by comparing a physical count of inventory with the Merchandise Inventory account balance. Shrinkage is normally charged to Cost of Goods Sold.

Learning Objective 8:

Analyze and interpret cost flows and operating activities of a merchandising company.

Summary

Net costs of merchandise purchases flows into Merchandise Inventory and from there to Cost of Goods Sold on the income statement. Any remaining Merchandise Inventory balance is reported as a current asset on the balance sheet. This is the beginning inventory for the next period.

Learning Objective 9:

Define and prepare multiple-step and single-step income statements.

Summary

Multiple-step income statements include greater detail for sales and expenses than do single-step income statements. Classified multiple-step income statements are usually limited to internal use. It shows more details, including computations of net sales and cost of goods sold, and reporting of expenses in categories reflecting different activities. Income statements published for external parties can be either multiple-step or single-step.

Learning Objective 10:

Prepare closing entries for a merchandising company.

Summary

Temporary accounts of merchandising companies include Sales, Sales Discounts, Sales Returns and Allowances, and Cost of Goods Sold. Each is closed to Income Summary.

Learning Objective 11 (Appendix 6A):

Record and compare merchandising transactions using both periodic and perpetual inventory systems.

Summary

Transactions involving the sale and purchase of merchandise are recorded and analyzed under both inventory systems. Adjusting and closing entries for both inventory systems are also illustrated and explained.

Learning Objective 12 (Appendix 6A):

Compute the gross margin ratio and explain its use as an indicator of profitability.

Summary

The gross margin (or gross profit) ratio is computed as gross margin (net sales minus cost of goods sold) divided by net sales. It is an indicator of a company's profitability before deducting operating expenses. A gross margin ratio must be large enough to cover operating expenses and give an adequate net income.

I. **Merchandising Activities**

    A. Reporting Financial Performance—revenue (*net sales*) from selling merchandise minus the cost of merchandise (goods) sold to customers is called *gross profit (gross margin)*. This amount minus operating expenses determines the net income or loss for the period.

    B. Reporting Financial Condition—Balance sheet includes one additional *current* asset called:

        1. *Merchandise Inventory*—or *inventory*, refers to products a company owns for the purpose of selling to customers.

        2. The cost of this asset includes the cost incurred to buy the goods, ship them to the store, and other costs necessary to make them ready for sale.

    C. Operating Cycle—begins with the purchase of merchandise and ends with the collection of cash from the sale of merchandise.

    D. Inventory Systems—two systems used to collect information about *cost of goods sold* and cost of inventory on hand.

        1. *Perpetual inventory system*—gives a continual record of the amount of inventory on hand. Accumulates the net cost of merchandise purchases in the inventory account and transfers the cost of each sale from the same inventory account to cost of goods sold when an item is sold

        2. *Periodic inventory systems*—requires updating the inventory account only at the end of a period to reflect the quantity and cost of both goods on hand and goods sold. Does not require continual updating of the inventory account. Records the cost of new merchandise in a temporary expense account called *purchases.*

    Note: This outline, except for Appendix 6A, outlines a Perpetual Inventory System. The terms Merchandise Inventory and Inventory are synonymous. Inventory is used for brevity.

II. **Accounting for Merchandise Purchases**—Perpetual Inventory System

    A. Purchase Returns and Allowances

        1. *Purchase returns* are merchandise received by a purchaser but returned to the supplier.

        2. A *purchase allowance* is a reduction in the cost of defective merchandise received by a purchaser from a supplier.

        3. A *debit memorandum* a document prepared by the purchaser to "debit" or reduce the purchaser's account payable.

        4. Entry: Debit Accounts Payable or Cash (if refund given) and Credit Inventory.

B. Trade Discounts—Deductions from list price (catalogue price) to arrive at the intended selling price. Trade discounts are not entered into accounts. Transactions are recorded using invoice price.

C. Purchase Discounts—Cash discounts granted to buyers for payment within a specified period of time called the discount period.

   1. Example : 2/10 n/30, offer a 2% discount if invoice is paid within 10 days of invoice date; net amount due in 30 days.

   2. Example: n/EOM (end of month): net amount due in 30 days.

   3. Entry for payment within discount period:
   Debit Accounts Payable (full invoice amount), Credit Cash (amount paid = invoice – discount), Credit Merchandise Inventory (amount of discount).

D. Managing Discounts—Most companies set up a system to pay invoices with favourable discounts within the discount period, preferably on the last day of a discount period. Missing out on cash discounts can be very costly.

E. Transfer of Ownership—defined by term:

   1. FOB (*free on board*) shipping point—ownership transfers at shipping point.

   2. FOB destination—buyer accepts ownership at the seller's place of business.

   3. Responsibility for transportation costs follows title or ownership.

F. Transportation Costs

   1. Shipping costs on purchases; called *transportation-in* or *freight-in*: include these as part of the cost of merchandise inventory if paid by company.

   2. Shipping goods to customers: called *transportation-out* or *freight-out*: record as delivery expense (a selling expense).

      a. Debit Merchandise Inventory, Credit Cash.

H. Recording Purchases Information—the net cost of merchandise purchased according to the *cost principle,* is recorded in the inventory account. (Inventory is debited or increased for invoice and transportation-in costs, and credited or reduced for returns, allowances and discounts.)

III. **Accounting for Merchandise Sales**—Perpetual Inventory System

    A. Sales Transactions—Recording has two parts:

        1. Account for revenue—Debit Accounts Receivable (or cash), Credit Sales (both for the invoice amount).

        2. Recognize cost—Debit Cost of Goods Sold, Credit Merchandise Inventory (both for the cost of the inventory sold).

    B. Sales Discounts—cash discounts granted to customers for payment within the discount period. Recorded upon collection for sale.

        1. Collection after discount period—Debit Cash, Credit Accounts Receivable (full invoice amount).

        2. Collection within discount period—Debit Cash (invoice amount less discount), Debit Sales Discount (discount amount), Credit Accounts Payable (invoice amount).

        3. Sales Discount is a contra-revenue account—subtraction from Sales.

    C. Sales Returns and Allowances

        1. *Sales returns*—merchandise customers return to the seller after a sale.

        2. *Sales allowances*—reductions in the selling price of merchandise sold to customers (usually for damaged merchandise that a customer is willing to purchase if the selling price is decreased).

        3. Entry: Debit Sales Returns and Allowances and Credit Accounts Receivable.
        Additional entry if returned merchandise is salable:
        Debit Inventory, Credit Cost of Goods Sold.

        4. Sales Returns and Allowances, and Sales Discounts, are contra-revenue accounts—subtract from Sales.

        5. Net Sales = Sales – (Sales Discount + Sales Returns and Allowances).

        6. *Credit memorandum*: prepared by the seller to "credit" or reduce the customer's accounts receivable.

IV.   **Adjustments**—Perpetual Inventory System

    A. Adjusting Entries—Generally same as service business.

        1. Additional adjustment needed for any inventory loss referred to as *shrinkage*.

        2. Shrinkage is determined by comparing a physical count of the inventory with recorded quantities.

        3. Entry: Debit Cost of Goods Sold, Credit Merchandise Inventory.

    B. Merchandising Cost Flow—Net purchases flows into Merchandise Inventory, from there to Cost of Goods Sold on the income statement. Remaining Inventory balance is reported on the balance sheet and becomes beginning inventory for the next period.

V.   **Income Statement Formats**—Perpetual Inventory System. No specific format is required in practice. Two common formats:

    A. Multiple-Step—more detailed than a listing of revenues minus expenses. Shows gross profit as a step towards determining net income. Two types:

        1. Classified Multiple-step—shows details of net sales. Calculates gross profit, and classifies expenses into selling and general, and administrative, calculates income from operations, reports other revenues and expenses, and calculates net income.

        2. Condensed Multiple-step—does not show details.

    B. Single-Step—includes cost of goods sold as an operating expense and shows only one subtotal for total expenses, one subtraction to arrive at net income.

VI.   **Closing Entries**—Perpetual Inventory System

    A. Similar for merchandising and service companies. Difference: must close temporary accounts related to merchandising activities.

        1. Debit balance temporary accounts, including sales discounts, sales returns and allowances, to Income Summary.

        2. All other closing entries same as for service companies.

Chapter Outline

VII. **Periodic and Perpetual Inventory Systems: Accounting Comparisons (Appendix 6A)**

   A. Periodic inventory system: merchandise inventory account is updated only once each accounting, at the end of the period.

   B. Records merchandise acquisitions, discounts and returns in temporary accounts (Purchases, Purchase Returns, Purchase Discounts).

   C. The inventory account can be updated as part of the adjusting or closing process.

   D. Requires closing additional temporary accounts.

VIII. **Using the Information**

   A. Gross Margin Ratio: the relation between sales and cost of goods sold; a major part of profit

      1. Calculated as: $\dfrac{\text{Gross Margin}}{\text{Net Sales}}$

      2. Represents the gross margin in each dollar of sales.

Z-MART
Income Statement
For the Year Ended December 31, 2001

Sales	....		$321,000
Less:	Sales discounts.................................	4,300	
	Sales returns and allowances..........	2,000	6,300
Net sales...			$314,700
Cost of goods sold			
Merchandise inventory, December 31,2000...		$ 19,000	
Purchases..	$235,800		
Less: Purchase returns and			
allowances $1,500			
Purchase discounts....................4,200	5,700		
Net purchases.....................................	$230,100		
Add: Transportation-in	2,300		
Cost of goods purchased		232,400	
Goods available for sale......................		$251,400	
Merchandise inventory, December 31, 2001 ..		21,000	
Cost of goods sold................................			230,400
Gross profit from sales...............................			$ 84,300
Operating expenses			
Selling expenses			
Amortization expense, store equipment	$ 3,000		
Sales salaries expense...................	18,500		
Rent expense, selling space.............	8,100		
Store supplies expense	1,200		
Advertising expense	11,300		
Total selling expenses...................		$42,100	
General and administrative expenses			
Amortization expense, office equipment	$ 700		
Office salaries expense..................	25,300		
Insurance expense........................	600		
Rent expense, office space	900		
Office supplies expense.................	1,800		
Total general and administrative			
expense	29,300		
Total operating expenses...........			71,400
Income from operations			$12,900
Other revenues and expenses			
Rent revenue..		$ 2,800	
Interest expense.....................................		(360)	2,440
Net income			$15,340

COMPONENTS OF NET INCOME (FROM OPERATIONS)

		Steps:
(a)	Net Sales	X
(b) −	Cost of Goods Sold*	− X
(c)	Gross Profit on Sales	X
(d) −	Operating Expenses	− X
(e)	Net Income (Loss) from Operations	X

COMPONENTS OF COST OF GOODS SOLD

		Steps:
(a)	Inventory, Beginning of Period	X
(b) +	Cost of Goods Purchased	+ X
(c)	Cost of Goods Available for Sale	X
(d) −	Inventory, End of Period	− X
(e)	Cost of Goods Sold	X

COMPONENTS OF COST OF GOODS PURCHASED

		Steps:
(a)	Purchases (Periodic Inventory System)	X
(b) −	Purchase Returns & Allowances and Purchases Discounts (Periodic)	− X
(c)	Net Purchases (Periodic)	X
(d) +	Transportation In	+ X
(e)	Cost of Goods Purchased	X

* Perpetual Inventory Systems have a cost of goods sold account that continuously accumulates costs as items are sold. In a Periodic System this amount is calculated at end of period.

ACCOUNTS USED IN BASIC MERCHANDISING TRANSACTIONS
WITH A PERIODIC INVENTORY SYSTEM

ASSETS	LIABILITIES	REVENUES & CONTRA-REV.	COST & CONTRA-COST
Cash	Accounts Payable	Sales	Purchases
Dr. Bal.	Cr. Bal.	Cr. Bal.	Dr. Bal.
Accounts Receivable		Sales Returns & Allowances	Purchase Returns & Allowances
Dr. Bal.		Dr. Bal.	Cr. Bal.

EXPENSE

Merchandise Inventory	Delivery Expense	Sales Discounts	Purchase Discounts
Dr. Bal.	Dr. Bal.	Dr. Bal.	Cr. Bal.
			Transportation In
			Dr. Bal.

Note: All Problems assume a perpetual inventory system is used unless identified as an appendix problem. Appendix problem assumes a periodic inventory system.

Problem I

The following statements are either true or false. Place a (T) in the parentheses before each true statement and an (F) before each false statement.

1. ( ) Sales returns and allowances or discounts are not included in the calculation of net sales.
2. ( ) On a classified multiple-step Income Statement, ending merchandise inventory is subtracted from the cost of goods available for sale to determine cost of goods sold.
3. ( ) Net sales minus cost of goods sold is gross profit on sales.
4. ( ) The Balance Sheet for a merchandising business is generally the same as a service business with the exception of the addition of one account.
5. ( ) The gross margin ratio is calculated dividing gross margin by net sales.
6. ( ) A perpetual inventory system requires updating the merchandise inventory at the fiscal period end.
7. ( ) Cash discounts on merchandise purchased are debited to the merchandise inventory account.
8. ( ) Transportation costs on merchandise purchased are debited to the merchandise inventory account.
9. ( ) A debit or credit memorandum may originate with either party to a transaction, but the memorandum gets its name from the action of the selling party exclusively.
10. ( ) Recording the purchase of merchandise on account requires a debit to the merchandise inventory account and a credit to accounts payable.

Problem II

You are given several words, phrases, or numbers to choose from in completing each of the following statements or in answering the following questions. In each case select the one that best completes the statement or answers the question and place its letter in the answer space provided.

_____ 1. A method of accounting for inventories in which cost of goods sold is recorded each time a sale is made and an up-to-date record of goods on hand is maintained is called a:

    a. product inventory system.
    b. perpetual inventory system.
    c. periodic inventory system.
    d. parallel inventory system.
    e. principal inventory system.

_____ 2. Based on the following information, calculate the missing amounts.

Sales	$28,800	Cost of goods sold	?
Beginning inventory	?	Gross profit	$10,800
Purchases	18,000	Expenses	?
Ending inventory	12,600	Net income	3,600

    a. Beginning inventory, $16,200; Cost of goods sold, $12,600; Expenses, $1,800.
    b. Beginning inventory, $23,400; Cost of goods sold, $10,800; Expenses, $7,200.
    c. Beginning inventory, $9,000; Cost of goods sold, $14,400; Expenses, $3,600.
    d. Beginning inventory, $12,600; Cost of goods sold, $18,000; Expenses, $7,200.
    e. Beginning inventory, $19,800; Cost of goods sold, $25,200; Expenses, $14,400.

3. What is the effect on the income statement at the end of an accounting period in which the ending inventory of the prior period was understated and carried forward incorrectly?
   a. Cost of goods sold is overstated and net income is understated.
   b. Cost of goods sold is understated and net income is understated.
   c. Cost of goods sold is understated and net income is overstated.
   d. Cost of goods sold is overstated and net income is overstated.
   e. The errors of the prior period and the current period offset each other, so there is no effect on the income statement.

4. The following information is taken from a proprietorship's income statement. Calculate ending inventory for the business.

Sales	$165,250	Purchase returns	$ 390
Sales returns	980	Purchase discounts	1,630
Sales discounts	1,960	Transportation-in	700
Beginning inventory	16,880	Gross profit	58,210
Purchases	108,380	Net income	17,360

   a. $19,840.
   b. $22,080.
   c. $21,160.
   d. $44,250.
   e. Some other amount.

5. On July 18, Triple Digit Sales Company sold merchandise on credit, terms 2/10, n/30, $1,080. On July 21, Triple Digit issued a $180 credit memorandum to the customer of July 18 who returned a portion of the merchandise purchased. In addition to the journal entry that debits inventory and credits cost of goods sold what other journal entry is necessary to record the July 21 transaction?

a.	Accounts Receivable	180.00	
	Sales		180.00
b.	Sales Returns and Allowances	180.00	
	Accounts Receivable		180.00
c.	Accounts Receivable	900.00	
	Sales Returns and Allowances	180.00	
	Sales		1,080.00
d.	Sales	180.00	
	Accounts Receivable		180.00
e.	Sales Returns and Allowances	180.00	
	Sales		180.00

6. The following information is available from Foster Company

Sales	$110,400
Sales discounts	6,325
Sales returns and allowances	5,650
Merchandise inventory, December 31, 2000	25,000
Merchandise inventory, December 31, 2001	27,000
Purchases	63,000

   Foster's gross margin ratio is:
   a. 38.0%
   b. 44.7%
   c. 50.2%
   d. 57.1%
   e. 64.0%

Problem III

Many of the important ideas and concepts discussed in Chapter 6 are reflected in the following list of key terms. Test your understanding of these terms by matching the appropriate definitions with the terms. Record the number identifying the most appropriate definition in the blank space next to each term.

_____ Cash discount
_____ Classified, multiple-step income statement
_____ Cost of goods sold
_____ Credit memorandum
_____ Credit period
_____ Credit terms
_____ Debit memorandum
_____ Discount period
_____ EOM
_____ FOB
_____ General and administrative expenses
_____ Gross margin
_____ Gross margin ratio
_____ Gross profit
_____ List price

_____ Merchandise
_____ Merchandiser
_____ Merchandise inventory
_____ Periodic inventory system
_____ Perpetual inventory system
_____ Purchase discount
_____ Retailer
_____ Sales discount
_____ Selling expenses
_____ Shrinkage
_____ Single-step income statement
_____ Supplementary records
_____ Trade discount
_____ Wholesaler

1. The cost of merchandise sold to customers during a period.

2. A method of accounting that maintains continuous records of the cost of inventory on hand and the cost of goods sold.

3. The abbreviation for end-of-month, used to describe credit terms for some transactions.

4. Inventory losses that occur as a result of shoplifting and deterioration.

5. A reduction in the price of merchandise that is granted by a seller to a purchaser in exchange for the purchase paying within a specified period of time called the discount period.

6. Gross margin (net sales minus cost of goods sold) divided by net sales; also called gross profit ratio.

7. Products that a company owns for the purpose of selling them to customers.

8. Expenses that support the overall operations of a business and include the expenses of such activities as providing accounting services, human resource management, and financial management.

9. A register of information outside the usual accounting records and accounts; also called supplemental records.

10. The catalogue price of an item before any trade discount is deducted.

11. The time period that can pass before a customer's payment is due.

12. The abbreviation for free on board, the designated point at which ownership of goods passes to the buyer.

13. A reduction below a list or catalogue price that may vary in amount for wholesalers, retailers, and final consumers.

14. The difference between net sales and the cost of goods sold; also called gross profit.

15. A term used by a purchaser to describe a cash discount granted to the purchaser for paying within the discount period.

16. A "middleman" that buys products from manufacturers or other wholesalers and sells them to retailers or other wholesalers.

17. Products, also called goods, that a company acquires for the purpose of reselling them to customers.

18. An income statement format that shows intermediate totals between sales and net income and detailed computations of net sales and costs of goods sold.

19. The difference between net sales and the cost of goods sold; also called gross margin.

20. The description of the amounts and timing of payments that a buyer agrees to make in the future.

21. A middleman that buys products from manufacturers or wholesalers and sells them to consumers.

22. The expenses of promoting sales by displaying and advertising the merchandise, making sales, and delivering goods to customers.

23. The time period in which a cash discount is available and a reduced payment can be made by the buyer.

24. Earns net income by buying and selling merchandise.

25. An income statement format that includes cost of goods sold as an operating expense and shows only one subtotal for total expenses.

26. A notification that the sender has entered a credit in the recipient's account maintained by the sender.

27. A method of accounting that records the cost of inventory purchased but does not track the quantity on hand or sold to customers; the records are updated at the end of each period to reflect the results of physical counts of the items on hand.

28. A term used by a seller to describe a cash discount granted to customers for paying within the discount period.

29. A notification that the sender has entered a debit in the recipient's account maintained by the sender.

Fundamental Accounting Principles, 10th Canadian Edition

Problem IV

The following amounts appeared on King Variety Store's adjusted trial balance as of December 31, 2002, the end of its fiscal year:

	Debit	Credit
Cash	$ 4,000	
Merchandise inventory	15,000	
Other assets	8,000	
Liabilities		$ 4,000
Lionel King, capital		22,300
Lionel King, withdrawals	10,000	
Sales		80,000
Sales returns and allowances	600	
Cost of goods sold	47,700	
General and administrative expenses	8,000	
Selling expenses	13,000	
Totals	$106,300	$106,300

On December 31, 2001, the company's merchandise inventory amounted to $13,000. *Supplementary records of* merchandising activities during the 2002 year disclosed the following:

Invoice cost of merchandise purchases	$48,500
Purchase discounts received	900
Purchase returns and allowances received	400
Cost of transportation-in	2,500

Required

Required: Using the data above, complete the Income Statement for King Variety Store for December 31, 2002. Use the form provided on the following page.

Income Statement

For the Year Ended December 31, 2002

Revenue:								
Sales								
Less: Sales returns and allowances								
Net sales								
Cost of goods sold:								
Merchandise inventory, December 31, 2001								
Purchases								
Less: Purchases returns								
and allowances $_____								
Purchase discounts _____								
Net purchases								
Add: Transportation-in								
Cost of goods purchased								
Goods available for sale								
Merchandise inventory, December 31, 2002								
Cost of goods sold								
Gross profit from sales								
Operating expenses:								
Selling expenses								
General and administrative expenses								
Total operating expenses								
Net income								

Problem V

Use the adjusted trial balance presented above to prepare the closing entries for King Variety Store. Do not give explanations, but skip a line after each entry.

	GENERAL JOURNAL				Page 1
DATE	ACCOUNT TITLES AND EXPLANATION	P.R.	DEBIT		CREDIT

Problem VI

1. If a company determines cost of goods sold by counting the inventory at the end of the period and subtracting the inventory from the cost of goods available for sale, the system of accounting for inventories is called a(n)_____.

2. Trade discounts _____ (are, are not) credited to the Inventory account.

3. A reduction in a payable that is granted if it is paid within the discount period is a _____ discount.

4. A store received a credit memorandum from a wholesaler for unsatisfactory merchandise the store sent back for credit. The store should record the memorandum with a _____ (debit, credit) to its Inventory account and a _____ (debit, credit) to its Accounts Payable account.

5. The two common systems of accounting for merchandise inventories are the _____ inventory system and the _____ inventory system. Before the availability of computers, the _____ inventory system was most likely used in stores that sold a large volume of relatively low-priced items.

Problem VII (Appendix 6A)

The trial balance that follows was taken from the ledger of Wizard Hobbies at the end of its annual accounting period. Jules Wizard, the owner of Wizard Hobbies, did not make additional investments in the business during 2001.

WIZARD HOBBIES
Unadjusted Trial Balance
December 31, 2001

Cash	$1,840	
Accounts receivable	2,530	
Merchandise inventory	3,680	
Store supplies	2,070	
Accounts payable		$4,370
Salaries payable	—	—
Jules Wizard, capital		5,980
Jules Wizard, withdrawals	1,380	
Sales		14,260
Sales returns and allowances	1,150	
Purchases	5,750	
Purchase discounts		920
Transportation-in	1,150	
Salaries expense	4,370	
Rent expense	1,610	
Store supplies expense	—	—
Totals	$25,530	$25,530

Use the adjusting entry approach to account for merchandise inventories and prepare adjusting journal entries and closing journal entries for Wizard Hobbies using the following information:

a. Ending store supplies inventory, $1,150.

b. Accrued salaries payable, $690.

c. Ending merchandise inventory, $4,830.

DATE	ACCOUNT TITLES AND EXPLANATION	P.R.	DEBIT	CREDIT

Solutions for Chapter 6

Problem I

1. F		6. F	
2. T		7. F	
3. T		8. T	
4. T		9. F	
5. T		10. T	

Problem II

1. B
2. D
3. C
4. A
5. B
6. A

Problem III

Fundamental Accounting Principles, 10th Canadian Edition

Problem IV

KING VARIETY STORE
Income Statement
For the Year Ended December 31, 2002

Revenue:			
Sales		$80,000	
Less: Sales returns and allowances		600	
Net sales			$79,400
Cost of goods sold:			
Merchandise inventory, December 31, 2001		$13,000	
Purchases	$48,500		
Less: Purchases returns and allowances	$400		
Purchase discounts	900	1,300	
Net purchases		$47,200	
Add: Transportation-in		2,500	
Cost of goods purchases		49,700	
Goods available for sale		$62,700	
Merchandise inventory, December 31, 2002		15,000	
Cost of goods sold			47,700
Gross profit from sales			31,700
Operating expenses:			
Selling expenses		$ 8,000	
General and administrative expenses		13,000	
Total operating expenses			21,000
Net income			$10,700

Problem V

Dec. 31	Sales	80,000.00	
	Income Summary		80,000.00
31	Income Summary	69,300.00	
	Sales Returns and Allowances		600.00
	Cost of Goods Sold		47,700.00
	General and Administrative Expenses		8,000.00
	Selling Expenses		13,000.00
31	Income Summary	10,700.00	
	Lionel King, Capital		10,700.00
31	Violet Valentine, Capital	10,000.00	
	Lionel King, Withdrawals		10,000.00

Problem VI

1. periodic inventory system

2. are not

3. cash

4. credit, debit

5. periodic, perpetual, periodic

Problem VII (Appendix 6A)

Adjusting Entries

Dec. 31	Store Supplies Expense	920.00	
	Store Supplies		920.00
31	Salaries Expense	690.00	
	Salaries Payable		690.00
31	Income Summary	3,680.00	
	Merchandise Inventory		3,680.00
31	Merchandise Inventory	4,830.00	
	Income Summary		4,830.00

Closing Entries

Dec. 31	Sales	14,260.00	
	Purchase Discounts	920.00	
	Income Summary		15,180.00
31	Income Summary	15,640.00	
	Sales Returns and Allowances		1,150.00
	Purchases		5,750.00
	Transportation-in		1,150.00
	Salaries Expense		5,060.00
	Rent Expense		1,610.00
	Store Supplies Expense		920.00
31	Income Summary	690.00	
	Jules Wizard, Capital		690.00
31	Jules Wizard, Capital	1,380.00	
	Jules Wizard, Withdrawals		1,380.00

Fundamental Accounting Principles, 10th Canadian Edition

CHAPTER 7
MERCHANDISE INVENTORIES AND COST OF SALES

Learning Objective 1:

Identify the items making up merchandise inventory.

Summary

Merchandise inventory comprises goods owned by a company and held for resale. Three special cases merit our attention. Goods in transit are reported in inventory of the company who holds ownership rights. Goods out on consignment are reported in inventory of the consignor. Goods damaged or obsolete are reported in inventory at a conservative estimate of their net realizable value, computed as sales price minus the selling costs.

Learning Objective 2:

Identify the costs of merchandise inventory.

Summary

Costs of merchandise inventory comprise expenditures necessary, directly or indirectly, in bringing an item to a saleable condition and location. This means the cost of an inventory item includes its invoice price minus any discount, plus any added or incidental costs necessary to put it in a place and condition for sale.

Learning Objective 3:

Compute inventory in a perpetual system using the methods of specific identification, weighted-average, FIFO, and LIFO.

Summary

Costs are assigned to the cost of goods sold account *each time* that a sale occurs in a perpetual system. Specific identification assigns a cost to each item sold by referring to its actual cost (for example, its net invoice cost). Weighted-average assigns a cost to items sold by taking the current balance in the merchandise inventory account and dividing it by the total items available for sale to determine the weighted-average cost per unit. We then multiply the number of units sold by this cost per unit to get the cost of each sale. FIFO assigns cost to items sold assuming earliest units purchased are the first units sold. LIFO assigns cost to items sold assuming the most recent units purchased are the first units sold.

Learning Objective 4:

Analyze the effects of inventory methods for financial reporting.

Summary

When purchase prices do not change, the choice of an inventory method is unimportant. But when purchase prices are rising or falling, the methods are likely to assign different cost amounts. Specific identification exactly matches costs and revenues. Weighted-average smoothes out price changes. FIFO assigns an amount to inventory closely approximating current replacement cost. LIFO assigns the most recent costs incurred to cost of goods sold, and likely better matches current costs with revenues.

Learning Objective 5:

Analyze the effects of inventory errors on current and future financial statements.

Summary

An error in the amount of ending inventory affects assets (inventory), net income (cost of goods sold), and owner's equity of that period. Since ending inventory is next period's beginning inventory, an error in ending inventory affects next period's cost of goods sold and net income. The financial statement effects of errors in one period are offset (reversed) in the next.

Learning Objective 6:

Compute the lower of cost or market amount of inventory.

Summary

Inventory is reported at market value when market is *lower* than cost. This is called the lower of cost or market (LCM) amount of inventory. Market may be measured as net realizable value or replacement cost. Lower of cost or market can be applied separately to each item, to major categories of items, or to the whole of inventory.

Learning Objective 7:

Apply both the gross profit and retail inventory methods to estimate inventory.

Summary

The gross profit method involves two computations: (1) net sales at retail multiplied by the gross profit ratio gives estimated cost of goods sold, and (2) goods available at cost minus estimated cost of goods sold gives estimated ending inventory at cost. The retail inventory method involves three computations: (1) goods available at retail minus net sales at retail gives ending inventory at retail, (2) goods available at cost divided by goods available at retail gives the cost to retail ratio, and (3) ending inventory at retail is multiplied by the cost to retail ratio to give estimated ending inventory at cost.

Learning Objective 8 (Appendix 7A):

Compute inventory in a periodic system using the methods of specific identification, weighted-average, FIFO, and LIFO.

Summary

Periodic systems allocate the cost of goods available for sale between cost of goods sold and ending inventory *at the end of a period*. Specific identification and FIFO give identical results whether the periodic or perpetual system is used. LIFO assigns cost to cost of goods sold assuming the last units purchased for the period are the first units sold. Weighted-average cost computes cost per unit by taking the total cost of both beginning inventory and net purchases and dividing by the total number of units available. It then multiplies cost per unit by the number of units sold to give cost of goods sold.

Learning Objective 9 (Appendix 7B):

Assess inventory management using both merchandise turnover and days' sales in inventory.

Summary

A high merchandise turnover is preferred provided inventory is not out of stock and customers are not being turned away. Days' sales in inventory is used to assess the likelihood of inventory being out of stock. A small number of days' sales in inventory is preferred provided we can serve customer needs and provide a buffer for uncertainties. These ratios help assess inventory management and evaluate a company's short-term liquidity.

Chapter Outline

I.   **Inventory Items and Costs**

    A. Merchandise Inventory—includes all goods *owned* by a company and held for sale.

        1. Goods in transit—included if ownership has passed (Terms: FOB shipping point).

        2. Goods on consignment—owned by consignor.

        3. Goods damaged or obsolete—included if salable at a conservative estimate of their *net realizable value* (sales price minus cost of making the sale).

    B. Costs of Merchandise Inventory—includes *all* expenditures necessary, directly or indirectly, in bringing an item to a saleable condition and location.

        1. Cost example: invoice price minus any discount, plus import duties, transportation-in, storage, insurance, etc.

        2. Exception: Under the *materiality principle* or the *cost-to-benefit constraint* (effort outweighs benefit), incidental costs of acquiring inventory may be immaterial and are then allocated to cost of goods sold in the period when they are incurred. Cost then equals invoice cost.

    C. Physical Count Merchandise of Inventory

        1. Generally taken at the end of its fiscal year or when inventory amounts are low (at least once per year).

        2. Used to adjust the Inventory account balance to the actual inventory on hand. Differences occur because of theft, loss, damage and errors.

II.   **Assigning Costs to Inventory**—Perpetual Inventory System

    A. Inventory Systems:

        1. Perpetual Inventory—Record cost of goods sold and reductions in inventory as sales occur; shown in chapter.

        2. Periodic Inventory— Determine cost of goods sold and inventory amounts at the end of a period; shown in appendix.

    B. Four methods of assigning costs to inventory and cost of goods sold:

        1. Specific Identification—assigns costs based on specific items identified.

        2. Weighted-Average—computes the average cost per unit of inventory at time of purchase.

        3. First-in, First-out (FIFO)—assumes inventory items are sold in the order acquired; costs of the earliest units purchased are charged to cost of goods sold, leaving costs of most recent purchases in inventory.

        4. Last-in, First-out (LIFO)—assumes that costs for the most recently purchased units are sold first and charged to cost of goods sold; earliest purchases are assigned to inventory.

C. Inventory Costing and Technology—advances in information and computing technology have reduced the cost of a perpetual inventory system. Timely access to information is being used strategically by companies to gain a competitive advantage.

III.   Inventory Analysis and Effects

A. Financial Reporting

1. The *materiality* principle states that an amount may not be ignored it its effect on the financial statements is important to their users.

2. The *full-disclosure principle (GAAP)* requires financial statements to report all relevant information about the operations and financial position the entity. The inventory costing method used must be disclosed in the notes to the financial statements.

B. When purchase prices are rising or falling, the inventory costing methods are likely to assign different cost amounts. Using *rising prices* as an example:

1. FIFO assigns the least (earlier) costs to cost of goods sold resulting in the highest gross profit and the highest net income. Advantage: Most current values are on the balance sheet as ending inventory. Disadvantage: Cost of goods sold does not reflect current costs therefore violates matching principle.

2. LIFO assigns the higher (later) amounts to cost of goods sold , yielding the lowest gross profit and the lowest net income. Advantage: Places the most current cost on the income statement as cost of goods sold. Disadvantage: LIFO is not accepted for tax purposes; ending inventory on the balance sheet is stated at the oldest costs.

3. Weighted-average method amounts fall between FIFO and LIFO. Advantage: Smoothes out purchase price changes. Disadvantages: Averaging does not accurately match expenses to revenues.

4. Specific identification costs depend on what units are actually sold. Advantage: Exactly matches costs and revenues. Disadvantages: Relatively more costly to implement and maintain.

    C. Consistency in Reporting Inventory

        1. *Consistency principle* requires use of the same accounting methods period after period so the financial statements are comparable across periods.

        2. Method change is acceptable if it will improve financial reporting. *The full-disclosure principle* requires that statement notes report type of change, its justification, and its effect on net income.

    D. Errors in Reporting Inventory

        1. Inventory errors cause misstatements in cost of goods sold, gross profit, net income, current assets, and owner's equity.

        2. Inventory errors yield opposite effects in cost of goods sold and net income. This ending inventory error carries over to the next period as a beginning inventory error, yielding a reverse effect.

        3. Because an inventory error causes an offsetting error in the next period, it is said to be *self-correcting*.

IV.   **Other Inventory Valuations**

    A. Lower of Cost or Market (LCM)— The conservatism principle requires that inventory be reported at market value when market is *lower* than cost.

        1. Market: defined as net realizable value (NRV) (selling price less any costs to sell), or current replacement cost.

        2. The decline from cost to market is recorded at the end of the period.

        3. Lower of cost or market is applied either:

           a. Separately to each individual item, or

           b. To major categories of items, or

           c. To the whole of inventory

    B. Gross profit method—estimates the cost of ending inventory by applying the gross profit ratio to net sales (at retail).

        1. Recognize the gross profit portion on each dollar of net sales.

        2. Calculate CGS percentage (100% less gross profit percentage)

        3. Sales multiplied by CGS percentage = CGS

        4. CGA – CGS = estimated ending inventory at cost

    C. Retail Inventory Method—estimates the cost of ending inventory for interim statements in a periodic inventory when a physical count is taken only annually. *Steps:*

        1. Subtract net sales at retail from goods available measured at retail price to get ending inventory at retail.

        2. Find cost to retail ratio by dividing cost of goods available at cost by goods available at retail.

        3. Apply cost ratio to ending inventory at retail to convert to ending inventory at cost.

Note: The cost to retail ratio is also used to convert a physical inventory taken using retail price to cost. Inventory shrinkage can be measured by comparing the converted physical inventory to the estimated inventory.

V. **Appendix 7A—Assigning Costs to Inventory—Periodic System**
   A. Results of periodic vs. perpetual by method:
      1. Specific Identification—results same as perpetual.
      2. Weighted-Average—calculations to determine weighted-average cost are performed with each purchase. Usually different results than perpetual.
      3. First-in, First-out (FIFO)—results same as perpetual.
      4. Last-in, First-out (LIFO)—results differ from perpetual because the timing of the cost assignment changes what is identified as the last cost.

VI. **Using the Information—Merchandise Turnover and Days' Sales in Inventory**
   A. Merchandise turnover
      1. The number of times a company turns over its inventory during a period
      2. Calculated as: $\dfrac{\text{Cost of goods sold}}{\text{Average merchandise inventory}}$
   B. Days' Sales in Inventory
      1. Estimates how many days it will take to convert inventory on hand into accounts receivable or cash.
      2. Calculated as: $\dfrac{\text{Ending inventory} \times 365}{\text{Cost of goods sold}}$

VISUAL #12

Schedule of Cost of Goods Available

	Units		Cost		Total
Jan. 1 Beginning Inventory	60	@	$10	=	$ 600
Mar. 27 Purchase	90	@	11	=	990
Aug. 15 Purchase	100	@	13	=	1,300
Nov. 6 Purchase	50	@	16	=	800
	300				$3,690

Cost of goods available for sale $3,690

Methods of Assigning Cost to Units in Ending Inventory

(1) **Specific Identification** — requires that each item in an inventory be assigned its <u>actual</u> invoice cost.

(2) **Weighted-Average** — a weighted-average cost per unit is determined based on total cost and units of goods available for sale. This cost is assigned to units in the ending inventory.

(3) **First-in, First-out (FIFO)** — assumes the first units acquired (beginning inventory) are the first to be sold and that additional sales flow is in the order purchased. Therefore, the costs of the last items received are assigned to the ending inventory.

(4) **Last-in, First-out (LIFO)** — assumes the last units acquired (most recent purchase) are the first units sold. Therefore, the cost of the first items acquired (starting with beginning inventory) are assigned to the ending inventory.

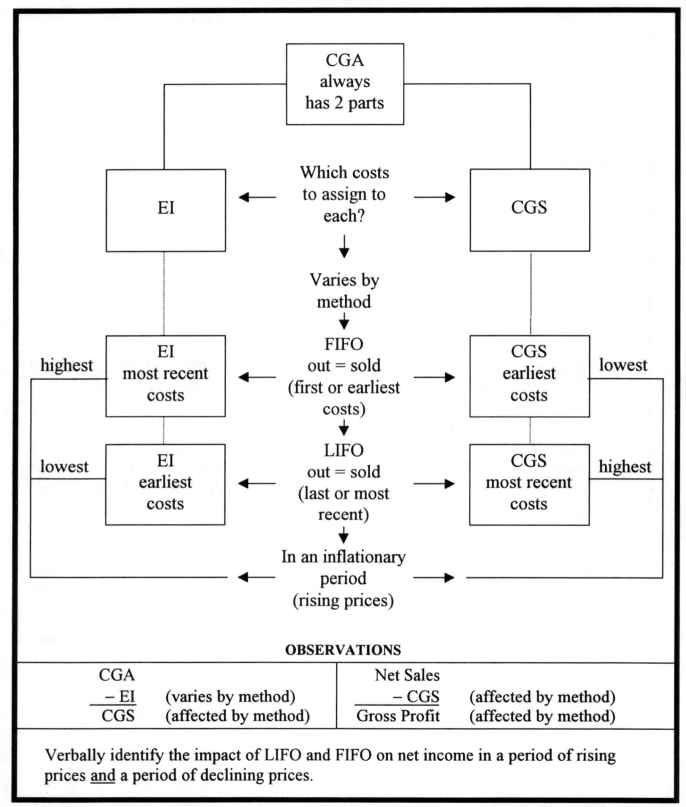

OBSERVATIONS

CGA		Net Sales	
− EI	(varies by method)	− CGS	(affected by method)
CGS	(affected by method)	Gross Profit	(affected by method)

Verbally identify the impact of LIFO and FIFO on net income in a period of rising prices <u>and</u> a period of declining prices.

Problem I

The following statements are either true or false. Place a (T) in the parentheses before each true statement and an (F) before each false statement.

1. ( ) The merchandise inventory of a business includes goods sold FOB destination if they are not yet delivered.

2. ( ) When a perpetual inventory system is used, the dollar amount of ending inventory is determined by counting the units of product on hand, multiplying the count for each product by Xs cost, and adding the costs for all products.

3. ( ) If prices of goods purchased remain unchanged, then all four methods of assigning costs to goods in the ending inventory would yield the same cost figures.

4. ( ) When first-in, first-out inventory pricing is used in a perpetual inventory system, as sales occur the costs of the first items purchased are assigned to cost of goods sold.

5. ( ) If prices are rising, then using the LIFO method of pricing inventory will result in the highest net income.

6. ( ) The conservatism principle supports the lower of cost or market rule.

7. ( ) A misstatement of ending inventory will carry forward and cause misstatements in the succeeding period's cost of goods sold, gross profit, and net income.

8. ( ) The perpetual inventory system uses a Purchases account to record items purchased.

9. ( ) Using FIFO, the perpetual and periodic inventory systems do not result in the same amounts of sales, cost of goods sold, and end-of-period merchandise inventory.

10. ( ) Lower of cost or market may be applied separately to each product, to major categories of products, or to the merchandise inventory as a whole.

Problem II

You are given several words, phrases, or numbers to choose from in completing each of the following statements or in answering the following questions. In each case select the one that best completes the statement or answers the question and place its letter in the answer space provided.

_____ 1.   Cisco Company's ending inventory consists of the following:

Product	Units on Hand	Unit Cost	NRV per Unit
X	100	$10	$ 8
Y	90	15	14
Z	75	8	10

Net realizable Value (NRV) is determined to be the best measure of market. Lower of cost or market for the inventory applied separately to each product is:

a. $2,950.
b. $2,810.
c. $2,660.
d. $3,100.
e. Cannot be determined from the information given.

The following information is to be used for questions 2 to 5:

Seneca Co. made purchases of a particular product in the current year (2001) as follows:

Jan.	1	Beginning inventory	120 units	@	$5.00	=	$ 600
Mar.	7	Purchased..................	250 units	@	$5.60	=	1,400
July	28	Purchased..................	500 units	@	$5.80	=	2,900
Oct.	3	Purchased..................	450 units	@	$6.00	=	2,700
Dec.	19	Purchased..................	100 units	@	$6.20	=	620
		Total	1,420 units				$8,220

Seneca Co. made sales on the following dates at $15 a unit:

Jan.	10	70 units
Mar.	15	125 units
Oct.	5	600 units
Total		795 units

The business uses a perpetual inventory system, and the ending inventory consists of 625 units, 500 from the July 28 purchase and 125 from the Oct. 3 purchase.

_____ 2. Using the specific identification cost assignment method, the amounts to be assigned to cost of goods sold and ending inventory respectively are:

    a. $4,465, $3,755

    b. $4,537.50, $3,682.50

    c. $4,570, $3,650

    d. $4,620, $3,600

    e. None of the above.

_____ 3. Using the LIFO cost assignment method, the amounts to be assigned to cost of goods sold and ending inventory respectively are:

    a. $4,465, $3,755

    b. $4,537.50, $3,682.50

    c. $4,570, $3,650

    d. $4,620, $3,600

    e. None of the above.

_____ 4. Using the FIFO cost assignment method, the amounts to be assigned to cost of goods sold and ending inventory respectively are:

    a. $4,465, $3,755

    b. $4,537.50, $3,682.50

    c. $4,570, $3,650

    d. $4,620, $3,600

    e. None of the above.

_____ 5. Using the weighted-average cost assignment method, the amounts to be assigned to cost of goods sold and ending inventory respectively are:

    a. $4,465, $3,755

    b. $4,537.50, $3,682.50

    c. $4,570, $3,650

    d. $4,620, $3,600

    e. None of the above.

Fundamental Accounting Principles, 10th Canadian Edition

_____ 6. Boston Company uses a perpetual inventory system and made an error at the end of year 1 that caused Atlantis' year 1 ending inventory to be overstated by $5,000. What effect does this error have on the company's financial statements?

a. Net income is understated; assets are understated.

b. Net income is understated; assets are overstated.

c. Net income is overstated; assets are understated.

d. Net income is overstated; assets are overstated.

e. Net income is overstated; assets are correctly stated.

_____ 7. Sharone Company wants to prepare interim financial statements for the first quarter of 2001. The company uses a periodic inventory system and has an average gross profit rate of 30%. Based on the following information, use the gross profit method to prepare an estimate of the March 31 inventory.

January 1, beginning inventory	$ 97,000
Purchases..	214,000
Purchase returns...	2,000
Transportation-in	4,000
Sales...	404,000
Sales returns	5,000

a. $ 33,700.

b. $193,300.

c. $119,700.

d. $179,900.

e. $ 26,700.

_____ 8. Cypress Company's ending inventory at December 31, 2002 and 2001, was $210,000 and $146,000, respectively. Cost of goods sold for 2002 was $832,000 and $780,000 for 2001. Calculate Cypress' merchandise turnover for 2002.

a. 4.7 times.

b. 4.5 times.

c. 4.0 times.

d. 3.8 times.

e. Cannot be determined from the information given.

_____ 9. Refer to the information presented in question 8. Calculate Cypress" days' sales in inventory for 2002.

a. 78.1 days.

b. 80.6 days.

c. 66.1 days.

d. 92.1 days.

e. 68.3 days.

Note: Questions 10–13 relate to Appendix 7A.

_____ 10. Magnum Company began a year and purchased merchandise as follows:

Jan.	1	Beginning inventory	40 units	@ $17.00
Feb.	4	Purchased	80 units	@ $16.00
May	12	Purchased	80 units	@ $16.50
Aug.	9	Purchased	60 units	@ $17.50
Nov.	23	Purchased	100 units	@ $18.00

The company uses a periodic inventory system and the ending inventory consists of 60 units, 20 from each of the last three purchases. Determine ending inventory assuming costs are assigned on the basis of FIFO.

a. $1,040

b. $1,000

c. $1,069

d. $1,080

e. $1,022

_____ 11. Linder Company began a year and purchased merchandise as follows:

Jan.	1	Beginning inventory	40 units	@ $17.00
Feb.	4	Purchased	80 units	@ $16.00
May	12	Purchased	80 units	@ $16.50
Aug.	9	Purchased	60 units	@ $17.50
Nov.	23	Purchased	100 units	@ $18.00

The company uses a periodic inventory system and the ending inventory consists of 60 units, 20 from each of the last three purchases. Determine ending inventory assuming costs are assigned on the basis of LIFO.

a. $1,040.

b. $1,000.

c. $1,022.

d. $980.

e. $1,080.

_____ 12. Box Company began a year and purchased merchandise as follows:

Jan.	1	Beginning inventory	40 units	@ $17.00
Feb.	4	Purchased	80 units	@ $16.00
May	12	Purchased	80 units	@ $16.50
Aug.	9	Purchased	60 units	@ $17.50
Nov.	23	Purchased	100 units	@ $18.00

The company uses a periodic inventory system and the ending inventory consists of 60 units, 20 from each of the last three purchases. Determine ending inventory assuming costs are assigned on the basis of specific invoice prices.

a. $1,000.

b. $1,022.

c. $1,040.

d. $1,080.

e. $990.

_____ 13. Crow Company began a year and purchased merchandise as follows:

Jan.	1	Beginning inventory	40 units	@ $17.00
Feb.	4	Purchased.......................................	80 units	@ $16.00
May	12	Purchased.......................................	80 units	@ $16.50
Aug.	9	Purchased.......................................	60 units	@ $17.50
Nov.	23	Purchased.......................................	100 units	@ $18.00

The company uses a periodic inventory system and the ending inventory consists of 60 units, 20 from each of the last three purchases. Determine ending inventory assuming costs are assigned on a weighted-average basis.

a. $1,022.00
b. $1,040.00
c. $1,080.00
d. $1,000.00
e. $1,042.50

Problem III

Many of the important ideas and concepts discussed in Chapter 7 are reflected in the following list of key terms. Test your understanding of these terms by matching the appropriate definitions with the terms. Record the number identifying the most appropriate definition in the blank space next to each term.

_____ Average-cost method
_____ Conservatism principle
_____ Consignee
_____ Consignor
_____ Consistency principle
_____ Days' sales in inventory
_____ First-in, first-out inventory pricing (FIFO)
_____ Full-disclosure
_____ Gross profit method
_____ Gross profit ratio
_____ Last-in, first-out inventory pricing (LIFO)

_____ Lower of cost or market (LCM)
_____ Materiality
_____ Merchandise turnover
_____ Net realizable value
_____ Physical count
_____ Replacement cost
_____ Retail
_____ Retail inventory method
_____ Specific identification method
_____ Specific invoice inventory pricing
_____ Weighted-average inventory pricing

1. Another name for specific invoice inventory pricing.

2. The pricing of an inventory under the assumption that inventory items are sold in the order acquired; the first items received were the first items sold.

3. This GAAP states that an amount may be ignored if its effect on the financial statements is not important to their users.

4. A procedure for estimating an ending inventory in which the past gross profit rate is used to estimate cost of goods sold, which is then subtracted from the cost of goods available for sale to determine the estimated ending inventory.

5. The pricing of an inventory under the assumption that the most recent items purchased are sold first and their costs are charged to cost of goods sold.

6. To count merchandise inventory for the purpose of reconciling goods actually on hand to the inventory control account in the general ledger.

7. The pricing of an inventory where the purchase invoice of each item in the ending inventory is identified and used to determine the cost assigned to the inventory.

8. The GAAP that requires financial statements (including footnotes) to report all relevant information about the operations and financial position of the entity.

9. An estimate of how many days it will take to convert the inventory on hand at the end of the period into accounts receivable or cash; calculated by dividing the ending inventory by cost of goods sold and multiplying the result by 365.

10. The required method of reporting merchandise inventory in the balance sheet where market value is reported when market is lower than cost; the market value may be defined as net realizable value or current replacement cost on the date of the balance sheet.

11. One who receives and holds goods owned by another party for the purpose of selling the goods for the owner.

12. An inventory pricing system in which the unit prices of the beginning inventory and of each purchase are weighted by the number of units in the beginning inventory and each purchase. The total of these amounts is then divided by the total number of units available for sale to find the unit cost of the ending inventory and of the units that were sold.

13. Another name for weighted average inventory.

14. Measures how much of net sales is gross profit. Calculated as gross profit divided by net sales; also known as the gross margin ratio.

15. The accounting principle that guides accountants to select the less optimistic estimate when two estimates of amounts to be received or paid are about equally likely.

16. The expected sales price of an item minus the cost of making the sale.

17. The number of times a company's average inventory was sold during an accounting period, calculated by dividing cost of goods sold by the average merchandise inventory balance.

18. A method for estimating an ending inventory cost based on the ratio of the amount of goods for sale at cost to the amount of goods for sale at market selling prices.

19. An owner of goods who ships them to another party who will then sell the goods for the owner.

20. Current cost of purchasing an item.

21. The accounting requirement that a company use the same accounting methods period after period so that the financial statements of succeeding periods will be comparable.

22. The selling price of merchandise inventory.

Problem IV

Complete the following by filling in the blanks.

1. Consistency in the use of an inventory costing method is particularly important if there is to be

   _____.

2. If a running record is maintained for each inventory item of the number of units received as units are received, the number of units sold as units are sold, and the number of units remaining after each receipt or sale, the inventory system is called _____.

3. When a company changes its accounting procedures, the _____ principle requires that the nature of the change, justification for the change, and the effect of the change on _____ be disclosed in the notes accompanying the financial statements.

4. With a periodic inventory system, an error in taking an end-of-period inventory will cause a misstatement of periodic net income for _____ (one, two) accounting periods because _____

_____

_____

_____.

5. When identical items are purchased during an accounting period at different costs, a problem arises as to which costs apply to the ending inventory and which apply to the goods sold. There are at least four commonly used ways of assigning costs to inventory and to goods sold. They are:

a. _____ ;

b. _____ ;

c. _____ ;

d. _____ .

6. A major objective of accounting for inventories is the proper determination of periodic net income through the process of matching _____ and _____. The matching process consists of determining how much of the cost of the goods that were for sale during an accounting period should be deducted from the period's _____ and how much should be carried forward as _____, to be matched against a future period's revenues.

7. Although changing back and forth from one inventory costing method to another might allow management to report the incomes it would prefer, the accounting principle of _____ _____ requires a company to use the same pricing method period after period unless it can justify the change.

8. In the gross profit method of estimating an ending inventory, an average _____ _____ rate is used to determine estimated cost of goods sold, and the ending inventory is then estimated by subtracting estimated _____ from the cost of goods available for sale.

9. In separating cost of goods available for sale into cost of goods sold and cost of goods unsold, the procedures for assigning a cost to the ending inventory are also the means of determining _____ _____ because whatever portion of the cost of goods available for sale is assigned to ending inventory, the remainder goes to _____.

10. Cost of an inventory item includes _____

_____

_____

_____.

11. Use of the lower-of-cost-or-market rule places an inventory on the balance sheet at a _____ figure. The argument in favour of this rule provides that any loss should be _____ in the year the loss occurs.

12. When recording a sale of merchandise using a _____ (perpetual, periodic) inventory system, two journal entries must be made. One entry records the revenue received for the sale and the second entry debits the _____ account.

Problem V

A company uses a perpetual inventory system and during a year had the following beginning inventory, purchases, and sales of Product Z:

Jan.	1	Inventory	200 units	@	$0.50 = $100
Mar.	15	Purchased	400 units	@	0.50 = 200
Apr.	1	Sold	300 units	@	
June	3	Purchased	300 units	@	0.60 = 180
July	1	Sold	200 units	@	
Oct.	8	Purchased	600 units	@	0.70 = 420
Nov.	1	Sold	500 units	@	
Dec.	15	Purchased	500 units	@	0.80 = 400

In the spaces below show the cost that should be assigned to the ending inventory and to the goods sold under the following assumptions:

	Portions Assigned to—	
	Ending Inventory	Cost of Goods Sold
1. A first-in, first-out basis was used to price the ending inventory	$	$
2. A last-in, first-out basis was used to price the ending inventory	$	$

Problem VI

The following end-of-period information about a store's beginning inventory, purchases, and sales is available.

	At Cost	At Retail
Beginning inventory	$ 9,600	$13,000
Net purchases	54,400	69,100
Transportation-in	1,680	
Net sales		69,000

The above information is to be used to estimate the store's ending inventory by the retail method.

1. The store had goods available for sale during the year calculated as follows:

	At Cost	At Retail
Beginning inventory	$	$
Net purchases		
Transportation-in		
Goods available for sale	$	$

2. The store's cost ratio was:.............................
   $_____ / $_____ × 100 = _____

3. Of the goods the store had available for sale at retail prices during the year, the following is gone because of sales at retail..

   Which left the store an estimated ending inventory at retail.. $_____

4. And when the store's cost ratio is applied to this estimated ending inventory at retail, the estimated ending inventory at cost is .... $_____

The store took a physical inventory and counted only $12,850 of merchandise on hand (at retail). Calculate the inventory shortage at cost.

Solutions for Chapter 7

Problem I

1. T	6. T
2. F	7. T
3. T	8. F
4. T	9. F
5. F	10. T

Problem II

1. C	8. A
2. C	9. D
3. D	10. D
4. A	11. B
5. B	12. C
6. D	13. A
7. A	

Problem III

Average-cost method 13
Conservatism principle 15
Consignee 11
Consignor 19
Consistency principle 21
Days' sales in inventory 9
FIFO inventory pricing 2
Full-disclosure 8
Gross profit method 4
Gross profit ratio 14
LIFO inventory pricing 5

Lower of cost or market (LCM) 10
Materiality 3
Merchandise turnover 17
Net realizable value 16
Physical count 6
Replacement cost 20
Retail 22
Retail inventory method 18
Specific identification method 1
Specific invoice inventory pricing 7
Weighted-average inventory pricing 12

Problem IV

1. comparability in the financial statements prepared period after period

2. a perpetual inventory system

3. full-disclosure, net income

4. two, the ending inventory of one period becomes the beginning inventory of the next

5. (a) specific invoice prices; (b) weighted-average cost; (c) first-in, first-out; (d) last-in, first-out

6. costs, revenues, revenues, merchandise inventory

7. consistency

8. gross profit, cost of goods sold

9. cost of goods sold, cost of goods sold

10. the invoice price, less the discount, plus any additional incidental costs necessary to put the item in place and in condition for sale

11. conservative, recognized

12. perpetual, cost of goods sold

Problem V

	Portions Assigned to—	
	Ending Inventory	Cost of Goods Sold
1.	$750	$550
2.	520	780

Problem VI

	At Cost	At Retail
Goods for sale...		
Beginning inventory	$ 9,600	$13,000
Net purchases	54,400	69,100
Transportation-in	1,680	
Goods available for sale	$65,680	82,100
Cost ratio: $65,680/$82,100 × 100 = 80%.....		
Net sales at retail		69,000
Ending inventory at retail		$13,100
Ending inventory at cost ($13,100 × 80%).....	$10,480	

Inventory shortage at cost:
$13,100 − $12,850 = $250
$250 × 80% = $200

CHAPTER 8
ACCOUNTING INFORMATION SYSTEMS

Learning Objective 1:

Explain the relationship of the Accounting Information system (AIS) to the Management Information System (MIS).

Summary

The MIS includes the subsystems of Finance, Sales and Marketing, Human Resources, Production, and Accounting. The purpose of information systems is to collect and process data based on inputs for the purpose of generating useful information to both internal and external users.

Learning Objective 2:

Explain the components, structure, and fundamental standards of Accounting Information Systems.

Summary

An AIS collects financial data and processes it through the relevant component: Accounts Payable, Accounts Receivable, Payroll, or a specialty component such as Capital Assets. Computers are invaluable tools in processing data efficiently and effectively. Accounting information systems are guided by five fundamental standards in carrying out their tasks: control, relevance, compatibility, flexibility, and cost-benefits standards.

Learning Objective 3:

Identify what technology-based systems have impacted accounting.

Summary

Source documents are evolving from paper-based to technology-based such as Debit card, Electronic Funds Transfer (EFT), and E-commerce transactions. General purpose accounting software is available for small to medium-sized businesses whereas large businesses purchase enterprise-application software programs that can be customized to fit the specific needs of their operation

Learning Objective 4:

Explain the goals and uses of special journals.

Summary

Special journals are used for recording and posting transactions of similar type, each meant to cover one kind of transaction. Four of the most common special journals are the Sales Journal, Cash Receipts Journal, Purchases Journal, and Cash Disbursements Journal. Special journals are efficient and cost effective tools in helping journalize and post transactions. Special journals also allow an efficient division of labour that is also an effective control procedure.

Learning Objective 5:

Describe the use of controlling accounts and subsidiary ledgers.

Summary

A General Ledger keeps controlling accounts such as Accounts Receivable or Accounts Payable, but details on individual accounts making up the controlling account are kept in a subsidiary ledger (such as an Accounts Receivable Ledger). The balance in a controlling account must equal the sum of its subsidiary account balances after posting is complete.

Learning Objective 6:

Journalize and post transactions using special journals.

Summary

Special journals are devoted to similar kinds of transactions. Transactions are journalized on one line of a special journal, with columns devoted to specific accounts, dates, names, posting references, explanations and other necessary information. Posting is threefold: (1) individual amounts in the Other Accounts column are posted to their general ledger accounts on a regular (daily) basis, (2) individual amounts in a column that is posted in total to a controlling account at the end of a period (month) are posted regularly (daily) to its account in the subsidiary ledger, and (3) total amounts for all columns except the Other Accounts column are posted at the end of a period (month) to their column's account title.

Learning Objective 7:

Prepare and test the accuracy of subsidiary ledgers.

Summary

Account balances in the General Ledger and its subsidiary ledgers are tested for accuracy after posting is complete. This procedure is twofold: (1) prepare a trial balance of the General Ledger to confirm debits equal credits, and (2) prepare a schedule of a subsidiary ledger to confirm the controlling account's balance equals the subsidiary ledger's balance. A schedule is a listing of accounts from a ledger with their balances and the sum of all balances.

Learning Objective 8 (Appendix 8A):

Journalize and post transactions using special journals in a periodic inventory system.

Summary

Transactions are journalized and posted using special journals in a periodic system. The methods are similar to those in a perpetual system. The primary difference is cost of goods sold and inventory do not need adjusting at the time of each sale. This normally results in the deletion of one or more columns in each special journal devoted to these accounts.

Chapter Outline

I. **Accounting Information Systems**

   A. Management Information Systems (MIS) —the vehicle within an organization designed to collect and process data for the purpose of providing information users. Subsystems are sales and marketing, production, finance, human resources, and accounting.

   B. Accounting Information Systems (AIS) —group of components that collects and processes raw financial data into timely, accurate, relevant, and cost-effective information to meet the purposes of internal and external users. Primary components are accounts payable, accounts receivable, and payroll. AIS structure depends on the requirements of the users.

   C. Computerized AIS has both advantages and disadvantages.

   D. AIS—System Standards:

      1. Control Standard—requires that an AIS to have internal controls, which allow managers to control and monitor activities.

      2. Relevance Standard—requires that an AIS report useful, understandable, timely and pertinent information for effective decision making.

      3. Compatibility Standard—requires that an AIS conform with a company's activities, personnel, and structure

      4. Flexibility Standard—requires that an AIS adapt to changes in the company, business environment, and needs of decision makers.

      5. Cost-Benefit Standard—requires the benefits from an activity in an AIS to outweigh the costs of that activity.

II. **Accounting and Technology**

   A. Source Documents—provide the basic information processed by accounting system.

   B. Computers—Hardware is the physical equipment in a computerized system. Software refers to the programs that direct the operations of computer hardware.

III. **Special Journals in Accounting**—Perpetual Inventory Systems

   A. General Journal—an all-purpose journal where we can record any transaction.

   B. Special Journal—used in recording and posting transactions of similar type. Reduces time and effort.

   C. Subsidiary Ledger—individual accounts with common characteristics.

      1. General Ledger—continues to keep a single controlling account for each subsidiary ledger.

2. The balance in the controlling account must equal the sum of the individual balances in the subsidiary ledgers. Common subsidiary ledgers are:

    a. Accounts Receivable Ledger—used to keep a separate account for each customer. Controlled by Accounts Receivable Control in the General Ledger.

    b. Accounts Payable Ledger—used to keep a separate account for each creditor. Controlled by Accounts Payable Control in the General Ledger.

    c. Inventory Ledger—used to keep a separate account for each type of inventory. Controlled by Inventory Control in the General Ledger.

D. Four common special journals:

1. Sales Journal—used to record sales of merchandise on credit only. A special Sales Returns and Allowances Journal can be used by a company with large numbers of these items..

    a. End of the period—The *total* sales amount is posted as a debit to Accounts Receivable and as a credit to Sales in the General Ledger. The *total* cost amount is posted as a debit to Cost of Goods Sold and as a credit to Inventory.

    b. Individual transactions are typically posted each day to customer accounts in the Accounts Receivable Ledger.

2. Cash Receipts Journal—records *all* receipts of cash. Must be a columnar journal because different accounts are credited when cash is received from different sources.

    a. Cash from credit customers—in payment of a customer's account. Cash and Sales Discounts (debits) and Accounts Receivable (credit) are recorded.

    b. Cash sales—the amount of the sale is recorded as Cash (debit) or Sales Discounts (debit), and Sales (credit). The cost of sales is recorded as Cost of Goods Sold (debit) and Inventory (credit).

    c. Only the *totals* of special columns are posted to the General Ledger.

    d. Cash from other sources—a separate column is used for receipts that do not occur often enough to warrant a separate column. These include borrowings, interest on account, or selling unneeded assets. The account numbers for individual posting are included.

3. Purchases Journal—used to record all purchases on credit.

    a. Uses a special column for Purchase debit and Accounts Payable credit. Separate columns may be established for other purchases on credit.

b. Only the *totals* of special columns are posted to the General Ledger. Amounts in "Other Accounts" columns are posted *individually*

c. Credits to the accounts of particular creditors are *individually* posted to the subsidiary Accounts Payable Ledger.

4. Cash Disbursements Journal—used to record all payments of cash.

    a. Cheque Register—a cash disbursements journal that has a column for cheque numbers.

    b. A separate Cash credit column is established. Only the *total* of this column is posted.

    c. Separate credit columns are established for Accounts Payable debit and Purchases Discounts credit. Only the *totals* of special columns are posted to the General Ledger.

    d. A column titled "Other Accounts—Debit" is used to record all other payments. Each debit in the Other Accounts column must be posted *individually*.

    e. Debits to the accounts of particular creditors are *individually* posted to the creditor's account in subsidiary Accounts Payable Ledger.

5. General Journal—used for adjusting, closing, and correcting, and for special transactions not recorded in special journals.

E. Sales Tax

1. For companies that collects *sales tax (PST)* or *goods and services tax (GST)* from customers, the Sales Journal and the Cash Receipts Journal usually have separate columns for recording the collection of these taxes.

2. For companies that pay GST on purchases, the Purchases Journal and the Cash Disbursements Journal usually have separate columns for recording the payment of these taxes.

E. Testing the ledger

1. Account balances in the General Ledger and subsidiary ledgers are tested for accuracy after posting is complete.

    a. Prepare a trial balance of the General Ledger to confirm debits equal credits. If equal, the accounts in the General Ledger are assumed to be correct.

    b. Test the subsidiary ledgers by preparing a schedule of accounts receivable, with the account balances and the sum of all balances.

    c. If this total equals the balance of the Accounts receivable controlling account, the accounts in the Accounts Receivable Ledger are assumed correct.

VI.   **Appendix 8A—Special Journals under a Periodic System**

   A. Under a Periodic System the Cash Receipts and Sales Journals do not require an additional column entitled "Cost of Goods Sold Dr., Merchandise Inventory Cr." The Periodic System does not record the increase in cost of goods sold and decrease in inventory at the time of sale. .

   B. Purchases Journal—In a Perpetual System, a column for "Merchandise Inventory Dr." is included. In a Periodic System, this column is replaced by "Purchases Dr."

   C. Cash Disbursements Journal—In a Perpetual System, a column for "Merchandise Inventory Cr." Is included for recording discounts. In a Periodic System, this column is replaced by a "Purchase Discounts Cr."

Problem I

The following statements are either true or false. Place a (T) in the parentheses before each true statement and an (F) before each false statement.

1. ( ) A Purchases Journal is used to record all purchases.

2. ( ) At month-end, the total sales recorded in the Sales Journal is debited to Accounts Receivable and credited to Sales.

3. ( ) Sales is a General Ledger account.

4. ( ) Transactions recorded in a journal do not necessarily result in equal debits and credits to General Ledger accounts.

5. ( ) If a general journal entry is used to record a sale on credit, the credit of the entry must be posted twice.

6. ( ) A Management Information System is the vehicle within an organization designed to collect and process data for the purpose of providing information to users.

7. ( ) The primary components within and Accounting Information System are sales and marketing, production, finance, human resources, and accounting.

Problem II

You are given several words, phrases or numbers to choose from in completing each of the following statements or in answering the following questions. In each case select the one that best completes the statement or answers the question and place its letter in the answer space provided.

_____ 1. A company that uses a Sales Journal, a Purchases Journal, a Cash Receipts Journal, a Cash Disbursements Journal, and a General Journal borrowed $1,500 from the bank in exchange for a note payable to the bank. In which journal would the transaction be recorded?

    a. Sales Journal.
    b. Purchases Journal.
    c. Cash Receipts Journal.
    d. Cash Disbursements Journal.
    e. General Journal.

_____ 2. A company that uses a Sales Journal, a Purchases Journal, a Cash Receipts Journal, a Cash Disbursements Journal, and a General Journal paid a creditor for office supplies purchased on account. In which journal would the transaction be recorded?

    a. Sales Journal.
    b. Purchases Journal.
    c. Cash Receipts Journal.
    d. Cash Disbursements Journal.
    e. General Journal.

_____ 3. A book of original entry designed and used for recording only a specified type of transaction is a:

    a. Cheque Register.
    b. Subsidiary Ledger.
    c. General Ledger.
    d. Special Journal.
    e. Schedule of Accounts Payable.

_____ 4. Disadvantages of using a computerized Accounting Information System are:

    a. Greater range and detail of outputs available.

    b. Financial information is immediately available for updating and reporting.

    c. Lower cost of processing each transaction.

    d. Costs related to crashed/crashing systems.

    e. Higher productivity for employees and managers.

Problem III

Many of the important ideas and concepts discussed in Chapter 8 are reflected in the following list of key terms. Test your understanding of these terms by matching the appropriate definitions with the terms. Record the number identifying the most appropriate definition in the blank space next to each term.

_____ Accounting information system	_____ Enterprise-application software
_____ Accounts payable ledger	_____ Flexibility standard
_____ Accounts receivable ledger	_____ Foot
_____ Cash disbursements journal	_____ GST (Goods and services tax)
_____ Cash receipts journal	_____ HST (Harmonized sales tax)
_____ Cheque register	_____ PST (Provincial sales tax)
_____ Columnar journal	_____ Purchases journal
_____ Compatibility standard	_____ Relevance standard
_____ Computer hardware	_____ Sales journal
_____ Computer software	_____ Schedule of accounts payable
_____ Controlling account	_____ Schedule of accounts receivable
_____ Control standard	_____ Special journal
_____ Cost-benefit standard	_____ Subsidiary ledger
_____ Crossfoot	

1. A general ledger account the balance of which (after posting) equals the sum of the balances of the accounts in a related subsidiary ledger.

2. A provincial tax collected by retailers on customer purchases.

3. The special journal that is used to record all payments of cash; also called cash payments journal.

4. A list of the balances of all the accounts in the Accounts Receivable Ledger that is summed to show the total amount of accounts receivable outstanding.

5. An information system standard requiring that an information system adapt to changes in the company, business environment, and needs of decision makers.

6. The people, records, methods, and equipment that collect and process data from transactions and events, organize them in useful forms, and communicate results to decision makers.

7. A listing of individual accounts with a common characteristic.

8. To add a column of numbers.

9. The programs that direct the operations of computer hardware.

10. A journal that is used to record all purchases on credit.

11. The special journal that is used to record all receipts of cash.

12. An information system standard requiring that the benefits from an activity in an accounting information system outweigh the costs of that activity.

13. A journal used to record sales of merchandise on credit.

14. The sales tax in the Atlantic Provinces which is a combination of the GST and PST.

15. The physical equipment in a computerized accounting information system.

16. An information system standard requiring that an accounting information system report useful, understandable, timely and pertinent information for effective decision-making.

17. Another name for a cash disbursements journal when the journal has a column for cheque numbers.

18. Programs that manage a company's vital operations which range from order-taking programs to manufacturing to accounting.

19. A subsidiary ledger listing individual credit supplier accounts.

20. A list of the balances of all the accounts in the Accounts Payable Ledger that is summed to show the total amount of accounts payable outstanding.

21. A journal with more than one column.

22. Any journal that is used for recording and posting transactions of a similar type.

23. An information system standard requiring that an accounting information system conform with a company's activities, personnel, and structure.

24. An information system standard requiring that an accounting information system aid managers in controlling and monitoring business activities.

25. A subsidiary ledger listing individual credit customer accounts.

26. To add debit and credit column totals and compare the sums for equality.

27. A federal tax on the consumer on almost all goods and services.

Problem IV

Complete the following by filling in the blanks.

1. An accounting information system is a group of components that collects and processes _____ into _____ information to meet the purposes of internal and external users.

2. Five fundamental standards of accounting information systems are:

   a. _____

   b. _____

   c. _____

   d. _____

   e. _____

3. When a company records sales returns with general journal entries, the credit of an entry recording such a return is posted to two different accounts. This does not cause the trial balance to be out of balance because_____
   _____.

4. Cash sales _____ (are, are not) normally recorded in the Sales Journal.

5. When special journals are used, credit purchases of store supplies or office supplies should be recorded in the_____.

6. The posting principle upon which a subsidiary ledger and its controlling account operate requires that the controlling account be debited for an amount or amounts equal to the sum of _____ _____ to the subsidiary ledger and that the controlling account be credited for an amount or amounts equal to the sum of _____ to the subsidiary ledger.

7. Cash purchases of store supplies or office supplies should be recorded in a(n)_____
   _____.

8. When a subsidiary Accounts Receivable Ledger is maintained, the equality of the debits and credits posted to the General Ledger is proved by preparing _____. At the same time the balances of the customer accounts in the Accounts Receivable Ledger are proved by preparing_____.

Problem V

Below are nine transactions completed by Citizen Company on September 30 of this year. Following the transactions are the company's journals with prior September transactions recorded therein.

Requirement One: Record the nine transactions in the company's journals.

Sept. 30   Received an $808.50 cheque from Ted Clark in full payment of the September 20, $825 sale, less the $16.50 discount.

30   Received a $550 cheque from a tenant in payment of his September rent.

30   Sold merchandise to Inez Smythe on credit, Invoice No. 655, $1,675.

30   Received merchandise and an invoice dated September 28, terms 2/10, n/60 from Johnson Company, $4,000.

30   Purchased store equipment on account from Olson Company, invoice dated September 30, terms n/10, EOM, $950.

30   Issued Cheque No. 525 to Kerry Meadows in payment of her $650 salary.

30   Issued Cheque No. 526 for $1,715 to Olson Company in full payment of its September 20 invoice, less a $35 discount.

30   Received a credit memorandum from Olson Company for unsatisfactory merchandise received on September 24 and returned for credit, $625.

30   Cash sales for the last half of the month totalled $9,450.50.

GENERAL JOURNAL

DATE	ACCOUNT TITLES AND EXPLANATION	P.R.	DEBIT	CREDIT

SALES JOURNAL

DATE		ACCOUNT DEBITED	INVOICE NUMBER	P.R.	Accts Receivable Dr. Sales Cr.				
2001 Sept. 3		N. R. Boswell	651	√	1	8	7	5	00
	15	Inez Smythe	652	√	1	5	0	0	00
	20	Ted Clark	653	√		8	2	5	00
	24	N. R. Boswell	654	√	2	2	5	0	00

PURCHASES JOURNAL

DATE		ACCOUNT	DATE OF INVOICE	TERMS	P.R.	ACCOUNTS PAYABLE CREDIT					PURCHASES DEBIT					OTHER ACCOUNTS DEBIT				
2001 Sept. 8		Johnson Company	Sept. 6	2/10, n/60	√	3	7	5	0	00	3	7	5	0	00					
	22	Olson Company	Sept. 20	2/10, n/60	√	1	7	5	0	00	1	7	5	0	00					
	24	Olson Company	Sept. 22	2/10. n/60	√	5	6	2	5	00	5	6	2	5	00					

CASH RECEIPTS JOURNAL

DATE	ACCOUNT CREDITED	EXPLANATION	P.R.	CASH DEBIT	SALES DISCOUNTS DEBIT	ACCOUNTS RECEIVABLE CREDIT	SALES CREDIT	OTHER ACCOUNT CREDIT
2001 Sept. 1	Rent Earned	Tenant's September rent	406	5 5 0 00				5 5 0 00
13	N.R. Boswell	Full payment of account	√	1 8 3 7 50	3 7 50	1 8 7 5 00		
15	Sales	Cash sales	√	9 0 0 0 00			9 0 0 0 00	

CASH DISBURSEMENTS JOURNAL

Page 7

DATE	CH. NO.	PAYEE	ACCOUNT DEBITED	P.R.	CASH CREDIT	PURCHASES DISCOUNTS CREDIT	OTHER ACCOUNTS DEBIT	ACCOUNTS PAYABLE DEBIT
19—								
Sept. 15	523	Kerry Meadows	Salaries Expense	622	6 5 0 0 00		6 5 0 0 00	
16		Johnson Company		√	3 6 7 5 00	7 5 00		3 7 5 0 00

Requirement Two: The individual postings from the journals of Citizen Company through September 29 have been made. Complete the individual postings from the journals.

Requirement Three: Foot and crossfoot the journals and make the month-end postings.

Requirement Four: Complete the trial balance and test the subsidiary ledgers by preparing schedules of accounts receivable and accounts payable.

ACCOUNTS RECEIVABLE LEDGER

N. R. Boswell
2200 Falstaff Street

DATE	EXPLANATION	P.R.	DEBIT	CREDIT	BALANCE
2001 Sept. 3		S-8	1 8 7 5 00		1 8 7 5 00
13		R-9		1 8 7 5 00	
24		S-8	2 2 5 0 00		2 2 5 0 00

Ted Clark
10765 Catonsville Avenue

DATE	EXPLANATION	P.R.	DEBIT	CREDIT	BALANCE
2001 Sept. 20		S-8	8 2 5 00		8 2 5 00

Inez Smythe
785 Violette Circle

DATE	EXPLANATION	P.R.	DEBIT	CREDIT	BALANCE
2001 Sept. 15		S-8	1 5 0 0 00		1 5 0 0 00

ACCOUNTS PAYABLE LEDGER

Johnson Company
118 E. Seventh Street

DATE	EXPLANATION	P.R.	DEBIT	CREDIT	BALANCE
2001 Sept. 8		P-8		3 7 5 0 00	3 7 5 0 00
16		D-7	3 7 5 0 00		- 0 -

Olson Company

788 Hazelwood Avenue

DATE	EXPLANATION	P.R.	DEBIT	CREDIT	BALANCE
2001 Sept. 22		P-8		1 7 5 0 00	1 7 5 0 00
24		p-8		5 6 2 5 00	7 3 7 5 00

GENERAL LEDGER

Cash   Account No. 101

DATE	EXPLANATION	P.R.	DEBIT	CREDIT	BALANCE

Accounts Receivable   Account No. 106

DATE	EXPLANATION	P.R.	DEBIT	CREDIT	BALANCE

Store Equipment   Account No. 165

DATE	EXPLANATION	P.R.	DEBIT	CREDIT	BALANCE

Accounts Payable   Account No. 201

DATE	EXPLANATION	P.R.	DEBIT	CREDIT	BALANCE

Rent Earned   Account No. 406

DATE	EXPLANATION	P.R.	DEBIT	CREDIT	BALANCE
2001 Sept. 1		R-9		5 5 0 00	5 5 0 00

Sales   Account No. 413

DATE	EXPLANATION	P.R.	DEBIT	CREDIT	BALANCE

Sales Discounts   Account No. 415

DATE	EXPLANATION	P.R.	DEBIT	CREDIT	BALANCE

Purchases   Account No. 505

DATE	EXPLANATION	P.R.	DEBIT	CREDIT	BALANCE

Purchases Discounts   Account No. 507

DATE	EXPLANATION	P.R.	DEBIT	CREDIT	BALANCE

Salaries Expense   Account No. 622

DATE	EXPLANATION	P.R.	DEBIT	CREDIT	BALANCE
2001 Sept. 15		D-7	6 5 0 00		6 5 0 00

CITIZEN COMPANY

Trial Balance

September 30, 2001

Cash		
Accounts receivable		
Store equipment		
Accounts payable		
Rent earned		
Sales		
Sales discounts		
Purchases		
Purchases discounts		
Salaries expense		

CITIZEN COMPANY

Schedule of Accounts Receivable

September 30, 2001

CITIZEN COMPANY

Schedule of Accounts Payable

September 30, 2001

Solutions for Chapter 8

Problem I

1. F

2. T

3. T

4. F

5. F

6. T

7. F

Problem II

1. C

2. D

3. D

4. D

Problem III

Accounting information system......................6

Accounts payable ledger.........................2001

Accounts receivable ledger 25

Cash disbursement journal...........................3

Cash receipts journal...............................11

Cheque register 17

Columnar journal 21

Compatibility standard 23

Computer hardware.....................................15

Computer software..9

Controlling account 1

Control standard 24

Cost-benefit standard 12

Crossfoot 26

Enterprise application software 18

Flexibility standard 5

Foot..8

GST (Goods and services tax)...................27

HST (Harmonized sales tax) 14

PST (Provincial sales tax)...........................2

Purchases journal..10

Relevance standard 16

Sales journal...13

Schedule of accounts payable....................20

Schedule of accounts receivable 4

Special journal..22

Subsidiary ledger 7

Problem IV

1. Raw financial data, timely accurate relevant and cost-effective.

2. Control Standard, Relevance Standard, Compatibility Standard, Flexibility Standard, Cost-benefit Standard

3. Only the balance of one of the accounts, the Accounts Receivable account, appears on the trial balance.

4. are not

5. purchases journal

6. the debits posted, the credits posted

7. Cash Disbursements Journal

8. a trial balance, a schedule of accounts receivable

Problem V

Sept 30   Accounts Payable—Olson Company .... 201/√   625.00
            Purchases Returns and Allowances 506   625.00

SALES JOURNAL   Page 8

DATE		ACCOUNT DEBITED	INVOICE NUMBER	P.R.	Accts Receivable Dr. Sales Cr.				
2001 Sept. 3		N. R. Boswell	651	√	1	8	7	5	00
	15	Inez Smythe	652	√	1	5	0	0	00
	20	Ted Clark	653	√		8	2	5	00
	24	N. R. Boswell	654	√	2	2	5	0	00
	30	Inez Smythe	655	√	1	6	7	5	00
	30	Totals.			8	1	2	5	00
					(106/413)				

PURCHASES JOURNAL   Page 8

DATE	ACCOUNT	DATE OF INVOICE	TERMS	P.R.	ACCOUNTS PAYABLE CREDIT				PURCHASES DEBIT				OTHER ACCOUNTS DEBIT			
2001 Sept. 8	Johnson Company	Sept. 6	2/10, n/60	√	3	7 5 0		00	3	7 5 0		00				
	22	Olson Company	Sept. 20	2/10, n/60	√	1	7 5 0		00	1	7 5 0		00			
	24	Olson Company	Sept. 22	2/10. n/60	√	5	6 2 5		00	5	6 2 5		00			
	30	Johnson Company	Sept. 28	2/10, n/60	√	4	0 0 0		00	4	0 0 0		00			
	30	Str Equip/Olsn Co.	Sept. 30	n/10, EOM	165√		9 5 0		00					9	5 0	00
	30	Totals				16	0 7 5		00	15	1 2 5		00	9	5 0	00
						(201)				(505)				(√)		

CASH RECEIPTS JOURNAL

DATE	ACCOUNT CREDITED	P.R.	CASH DEBIT	SALES DISCOUNT DEBIT	ACCOUNTS RECEIVABLE CREDIT	SALES CREDIT	OTHER ACCOUNTS CREDIT
2001 Sept. 1	Rent Earned	406	5 5 0 00				5 5 0 00
13	N. R. Boswell	√	1 8 3 7 50	3 7 50	1 8 7 5 00		
15	Sales	√	9 0 0 0 00			9 0 0 0 00	
30	Ted Clark	√	8 0 8 50	1 6 50	8 2 5 00		
30	Rent Earned	406	5 5 0 00				5 5 0 00
30	Sales	√	9 4 5 0 50			9 4 5 0 50	
30	Totals		22 1 9 6 50	5 4 00	2 7 0 0 00	18 4 5 0 50	1 1 0 0 00
			(101)	(415)	(106)	(413)	(√)

CASH DISBURSEMENTS JOURNAL

DATE	CH. NO.	PAYEE	ACCOUNT DEBITED	P.R.	CASH CREDIT	PURCHASES DISCOUNTS CREDIT	OTHER ACCOUNTS DEBIT	ACCOUNTS PAYABLE DEBIT
2001 Sept. 15	523	Kerry Meadows	Salaries Expense	622	6 5 0 00		6 5 0 00	
16	524	Johnson Company		√	3 6 7 5 00	7 5 00		3 7 5 0 00
30	525	Kerry Meadows	Salaries Expense	622	6 5 0 00		6 5 0 00	
30	526	Olson Company		√	1 7 1 5 00	3 5 00		1 7 5 0 00
30			Totals		6 6 9 0 00	1 1 0 00	1 3 0 0 00	5 5 0 0 00
					(101)	(507)	(√)	(201)

GENERAL LEDGER

Cash — No. 101

Date	Debit	Credit	Balance
Sept. 30	22,20016.50		22,20016.50
30		6,690.00	15,506.50

Accounts Receivable — No. 106

Date	Debit	Credit	Balance
Sept. 30	8,125.00		8,125.00
30		2,700.00	5,425.00

Store Equipment — No. 165

Date	Debit	Credit	Balance
Sept. 30	950.00		950.00

Accounts Payable — No. 201

Date	Debit	Credit	Balance
Sept. 30		16,075.00	16,075.00
30	5,500.00		10,575.00
30	625.00		9,950.00

Rent Earned — No. 406

Date	Debit	Credit	Balance
Sept. 1		550.00	550.00
30		550.00	1,100.00

Sales — No. 413

Date	Debit	Credit	Balance
Sept. 30		8,125.00	8,125.00
30		18,450.50	26,575.50

Sales Discounts — No. 415

Date	Debit	Credit	Balance
Sept. 30	54.00		54.00

Purchases — No. 505

Date	Debit	Credit	Balance
Sept. 30	15,125.00		15,125.00

Purchases Returns & Allowances — No. 506

Date	Debit	Credit	Balance
Sept. 30		625.00	625.00

Purchases Discounts — No. 507

Date	Debit	Credit	Balance
Sept. 30		110.00	110.00

Salaries Expense — No. 622

Date	Debit	Credit	Balance
Sept. 15	650.00		650.00
30	650.00		1,300.00

ACCOUNTS PAYABLE LEDGER

Johnson Company

Date	Debit	Credit	Balance
Sept. 8		3,750.00	3,750.00
16	3,750.00		-0-
30		4,000.00	4,000.00

Olson Company

Date	Debit	Credit	Balance
Sept. 22		1,750.00	1,750.00
24		5,625.00	7,375.00
30		950.00	8,325.00
30	1,750.00		6,575.00
30	625.00		5,950.00

ACCOUNTS RECEIVABLE LEDGER

N. R. Boswell

Date	Debit	Credit	Balance
Sept. 3	1,875.00		1,875.00
13		1,875.00	-0-
24	2,250.00		2,250.00

Inez Smythe

Date	Debit	Credit	Balance
Sept. 15	1,500.00		1,500.00
30	1,675.00	5,625.00	3,175.00

Ted Clark

Date	Debit	Credit	Balance
Sept. 20	825.00		825.00
30		825.00	-0-

CITIZEN COMPANY
Trial Balance
September 30, 2001

Cash	$15,506.50	
Accounts receivable	5,425.00	
Store equipment	950.00	
Accounts payable		$ 9,950.00
Rent earned		1,100.00
Sales		26,575.50
Sales discounts	54.00	
Purchases	15,125.00	
Purchases returns and allowances		625.00
Purchase discounts		110.00
Salaries expense	1,300.00	
Totals	$38,360.50	$38,360.50

CITIZEN COMPANY
Schedule of Accounts Receivable
September 30, 2001

N. R. Boswell	$2,250.00
Inez Smythe	3,175.00
Total accounts receivable	$5,425.00

CITIZEN COMPANY
Schedule of Accounts Payable
September 30, 2001

Johnson Company	$4,000.00
Olson Company	5,950.00
Total accounts payable	$9,950.00

CHAPTER 9
INTERNAL CONTROL AND CASH

Learning Objective 1:

Define and explain the purpose and identify the principles of internal control.

Summary

An internal control system is the policies and procedures that managers use to protect assets, ensure reliable accounting, promote efficient operations, and encourage adherence to company policies. It is a key part of systems design, analysis and performance. It can prevent avoidable losses and help managers both plan operations and monitor company and human performance. Principles of good internal control include establishing responsibilities, maintaining adequate records, insuring assets and bonding employees, separating recordkeeping from custody of assets, dividing responsibilities for related transactions, applying technological controls, and performing regular independent reviews.

Learning Objective 2:

Define cash and how it is reported.

Summary

Cash includes currency and coins, and amounts on deposit in bank, chequing and some savings accounts. It also includes items that are acceptable for deposit in these accounts. Cash equivalents or short-term investments are similar to cash, therefore most companies combine them with cash as a single item on the balance sheet. Cash and cash equivalents are liquid assets because they are converted easily into other assets or used in paying for services or liabilities.

Learning Objective 3:

Apply internal control to cash.

Summary

Internal control of cash receipts ensures all cash received is properly recorded and deposited. Cash receipts arise from many transactions including cash sales, collections of customers' accounts, receipts of interest and rent, bank loans, sale of assets, and owner investments. Attention is focused on two important types of cash receipts: over-the-counter and mail. The principles of internal control are applied in both cases. Good internal control for over-the-counter cash receipts includes use of a cash register, customer review, receipts, a permanent transaction record, and the separation of the custody of cash from its recordkeeping. Good internal control for cash receipts by mail includes at least two people assigned to open mail and prepare a list when money is received with each sender's name, amount, and explanation.

Learning Objective 4:

Explain and record petty cash fund transactions.

Summary

Petty cash disbursements are payments of small amounts for items such as postage, courier fees, repairs and supplies. To avoid writing cheques for small amounts, a company usually sets up one or more petty cash fund and uses the money to make small payments. A petty fund cashier is responsible for safekeeping of the cash, for making payments from this fund, and for keeping receipts and records. A Petty Cash account is debited when the fund is established or increased in size. The cashier presents all paid receipts to the company's cashier for reimbursement. Petty cash disbursements are recorded whenever the fund is replenished with debits to expense accounts reflecting receipts and a credit to cash. The petty cash fund is now restored to its full amount and is ready to cover more small expenditures.

Learning Objective 5:

Identify control features of banking activities.

Summary

Banks offer several basic services that promote either, or both, the control or safeguarding of cash. These involve the bank account, the bank deposit, and chequing. A bank account is a record set up by a bank permitting a customer to deposit money for safeguarding and cheque withdrawals. A bank deposit is money contributed to the account with a deposit ticket as proof. A cheque is a document signed by the depositor instructing the bank to pay a specified amount of money to a designated recipient. Electronic funds transfer uses electronic communication to transfer cash from one party to another, and it decreases certain risks while exposing others. Companies increasingly use it because of its convenience and low cost.

Learning Objective 6:

Prepare a bank reconciliation.

Summary

A bank reconciliation is prepared to prove the accuracy of the depositor's and the bank's records. In completing a reconciliation, the bank statement balance is adjusted for such items as outstanding cheques and unrecorded deposits made on or before the bank statement date but not reflected on the statement. The depositor's cash account balance also often requires adjustment. These adjustments include items such as service charges, bank collections for the depositor, and interest earned on the account balance.

Learning Objective 7 (Appendix 9A):

Apply the voucher system to control cash disbursements.

Summary

A voucher system is a set of procedures and approvals designed to control cash disbursements and acceptance of obligations. The voucher system of control relies on several important documents including the voucher and many supporting files. A voucher system's control over cash disbursements begins when a company incurs an obligation that will result in payment of cash. A key factor in this system is that only approved departments and individuals are authorized to incur certain obligations. To coordinate and control responsibilities of these departments, several different business documents are used.

Learning Objective 8 (Appendix 9B):

Compute the acid-test ratio and explain its use as an indicator of a company's liquidity.

Summary

The acid-test ratio is computed as quick assets (cash, short-term investments, and receivables) divided by current liabilities. It is an indicator of a company's ability to pay its current liabilities with its existing quick assets. A ratio equal to or greater than one is often considered adequate.

I.   **Internal Control**

    A. Purpose—An *internal control system* is all policies and procedures used to:

        1. Protect assets.

        2. Ensure reliable accounting.

        3. Promote efficient operations.

        4. Encourage adherence to company policies.

    B. Principles of Internal Control:

        1. *Establish responsibilities* for each task clearly and to one person.

        2. *Maintain adequate records to help protect assets* by ensuring that employees use prescribed procedures.

        3. *Insure assets and bond key employees* to reduce risk from casualty and theft.

        4. *Separate recordkeeping from custody of assets* so a person who controls or has access to an asset is not responsible for the maintenance of that asset's accounting records.

        5. *Divide responsibility for related transactions* between two or more individuals or departments; also called *separation of duties.*

        6. *Apply technological controls.*

        7. *Perform regular and independent reviews* to ensure internal control procedures are followed.

    C. Technology and Internal Control—fundamental principles of internal control are relevant no matter what the technological state of the accounting system. Some technological impacts we must be alert to:

        1. Reduced processing errors.

        2. More extensive testing of records.

        3. Limited evidence of processing.

        4. Crucial separation of duties.

    D. Limitations of Internal Control

        1. Human error.

        2. Human fraud.

Chapter Outline

II.   Cash—Definition and Reporting

    A. Cash—includes currency, coins, amounts on deposit in bank accounts, chequing accounts and some savings accounts.

    B. *Cash equivalents* are short-term investments, similar to cash.

    C. *Liquidity* refers to how easily an asset can be converted into another asset or be used in paying for services or obligations.

III.   Internal Control of Cash

    A. Internal cash control procedures should meet three guidelines:

        1. Separate handling of cash from recordkeeping of cash.

        2. Cash receipts are promptly (daily) deposited in a bank.

        3. Cash disbursements are made by cheque.

    B. Control of Cash Receipts—include procedures for protecting:

        1. Over-the-counter cash receipts

            a. Apply internal control principles, and

            b. Record cash shortages and overages.

        2. Cash receipts by mail.

    C. Control of Cash Disbursements—to safeguard against theft:

        1. Requires that all expenditures be made by cheque, with two signatures if possible when not signed by the owner, that person not having access to the accounting records.

        2. Exception—small payments made from *petty cash fund.* Use of petty cash fund involves:

            a. Debit to Petty Cash only when the fund is established or increased.

            b. Assign a petty cashier (custodian) to account for the amounts expended and keep receipts.

            c. Reimbursement—debit the expenses or other items paid for with petty cash and credit Cash for the amount reimbursed to the petty cash fund.

            d. Recording any petty cash shortages/overages.

IV.   Banking Activities as Controls

    A. Bank Account—permits the customer to deposit money for safeguarding and cheques for withdrawals.

    B. Electronic Funds Transfer (EFT)—use of electronic communication to transfer cash from one party to another.

    C. Bank Statement—shows the activity in the accounts during the month.

D. A *bank reconciliation* proves the accuracy of the depositor's cash records. The difference between the balance of cash according to the depositor's records and the balance reported on the bank statement is explained.

E. Factors causing the bank statement balance to differ from the depositor's book balance are:

1. Outstanding cheques.
2. Unrecorded deposits.
3. Deductions for uncollectible items and services
4. Additions for collections and interest.
5. Errors.

F. Bank Reconciliation—steps in reconciling:

1. Identify the bank balance of the cash account (*balance per bank*).
2. Identify and list any unrecorded deposits and any bank errors understating the bank balance. Add them to the bank balance.
3. Identify and list any outstanding cheques and any bank errors overstating the bank balance. Deduct them from the bank balance.
3. Compute the *adjusted bank balance*, also called corrected or *reconciled* balance.
4. Identify the company's balance of the cash account (*balance per book*).
5. Identify and list any unrecorded credit memoranda from the bank, interest earned, and errors understating the book balance. Add them to the book balance.
6. Identify and list any unrecorded debit memoranda from the bank, service charges, and errors overstating the book balance. Deduct them from the book balance.
7. Compute the *adjusted book balance*, also called corrected or reconciled balance.
8. Verify the two adjusted balances from steps 4 and 8 are equal. If yes, they are reconciled. If not, check for mathematical accuracy and missing data.

G. Recording adjusting entries from bank reconciliation

1. Additions to book balance are debits to cash. The credit account is dependent on the reason for the addition. Examples are notes collected by the bank and interest earned.

2. Subtractions from book balance are credits to cash. The debit account is dependent on reason for the subtraction. Examples are accounts receivable, for NSF cheques, and service charges.

V. **Voucher System of Control (Appendix 9A)**

A. A voucher system is a set of procedures and approvals designed to control cash disbursements and acceptance of obligations The voucher system of control establishes procedures for:

1.:

  a. Accepting obligations resulting in cash disbursements.

  b. Verifying, approving and recording obligations.

  c. Issuing cheques for payment of verified, approved and recorded obligations.

  d. Requiring obligations be recorded when incurred.

  e. Treating each purchase as an independent transaction

2. Business documents include:

  a. Purchase requisitions.

  b. Purchase orders.

  c. Invoices.

  d. Receiving reports.

  e. Invoice approval forms.

  f. The voucher

VI. **Using the Information — Acid-Test Ratio (Appendix 9B)**

A. Because merchandise inventories are not readily available as a source of payment for current liabilities, a measure other than the current ratio is used to obtain a more strict measure of a company's ability to cover current liabilities:

B. Acid-test ratio = $\dfrac{\text{Quick assets*}}{\text{Current liabilities}}$

  * Quick assets are cash, short-term investments, and receivables

BANK RECONCILIATION

Reasons for discrepancies between
bank statement balance and chequebook
balance:

	Handle as follows:
Unrecorded deposits	Add to bank balance
Outstanding cheques	Deduct from bank balance
Bank service charges	Deduct from book balance
Debit memos	Deduct from book balance
Credit memos	Add to book balance
NSF cheques	Deduct from book balance
Interest	Add to book balance
Errors	Must analyze individually (bank errors affect bank balance and book errors affect book balance)

Problem I

The following statements are either true or false. Place a (T) in the parentheses before each true statement and an (F) before each false statement.

1. ( ) One of the fundamental principles of internal control states that the person who has access to or is responsible for an asset should not maintain the accounting record for that asset.

2. ( ) Procedures for controlling cash disbursements are as important as those for cash receipts.

3. ( ) Cash includes currency, coins, and amounts on deposit in bank accounts.

4. ( ) In order to approve an invoice for payment for the purchase of assets, the accounting department of a large company should require copies of the purchase requisition, purchase order, invoice, and receiving report.

5. ( ) After the petty cash fund is established, the Petty Cash account is not debited or credited again unless the size of the fund is changed.

6. ( ) The Cash Over and Short account is usually shown on the income statement as part of miscellaneous revenues if it has a credit balance at the end of the period.

7. ( ) If 20 cancelled cheques are listed on the current month's bank statement, then no less than 20 cheques could have been issued during the current month.

8. ( ) If an error is made on the bank statement, then a journal entry is needed.

Problem II

You are given several words, phrases, or numbers to choose from in completing each of the following statements or in answering the following questions. In each case select the one that best completes the statement or answers the question and place its letter in the answer space provided.

_____ 1. One of the following is NOT a fundamental internal control principle:

   a. .Maintain adequate records.
   b. .Separate recordkeeping from custody of assets.
   c. Ensure adequate cash is available to pay liabilities.
   d. .Insure assets and bond key employees.
   e. Establish responsibilities for each task.

_____ 2. Liquidity is:

   a. The portion of a corporation's equity that represents investments in the corporation by its shareholders.
   b. Cash or other assets that are reasonably expected to be realized in cash or be sold or consumed within one year or one operating cycle of the business.
   c. A characteristic of an asset indicating how easily the asset can be converted into cash or used to buy services or satisfy obligations.
   d. Obligations that are due to be paid or liquidated within one year or one operating cycle of the business.
   e. Economic benefits or resources without physical substance, the value of which stems from the privileges or rights that accrue to their owner.

_____ 3.   The purpose of a bank reconciliation is to:

   a. Ensure that all transaction have been properly recorded.

   b. .Ensure that only authorized payments have been made.

   c. .Prove the accuracy of the depositor's cash records.

   d. Ensure the accuracy of the bank statement.

   e. .Ensure that all payments have been made by cheque.

_____ 4.   Each of the following items would cause Brand X Sales Company's book balance of cash to differ from its bank statement balance.

   A. A service charge made by the bank.

   B. A cheque listed as outstanding on the previous month's reconciliation and that is still outstanding.

   C. A customer's cheque returned by the bank marked "NSF."

   D. A deposit which was mailed to the bank on the last day of November and is unrecorded on the November bank statement.

   E. A cheque paid by the bank at its correct $422 amount but recorded in error in the General Journal at $442.

   F. An unrecorded credit memorandum indicating the bank had collected a note receivable for Brand X Sales Company and deposited the proceeds in the company's account.

   G. A cheque written during November and not yet paid and returned by the bank.

   Which of the above items require entries on the books of Brand X Sales Company?

   a. A, B, C, and E

   b. A, C, E, and F

   c. A, B, D, and F

   d. A, B, D, E, and G

   e. C, D, E. and F

   5   A company reported the following year-end account balances for 2002.

Cash	$22,000
Short-term investments	$15,000
Accounts receivable	$33,000
Merchandise Inventory	$45,000
Current liabilities	$78,000

   a. 0.28

   b. 0.47

   c. 0.90

   d. 1.11

   e. 1.47

Problem III

Many of the important ideas and concepts discussed in Chapter 9 are reflected in the following list of key terms. Test your understanding of these terms by matching the appropriate definitions with the terms. Record the number identifying the most appropriate definition in the blank space next to each term.

_____	Acid-test ratio	_____	Liquid asset
_____	Bank reconciliation	_____	Liquidity
_____	Bond	_____	Quick assets
_____	Cancelled cheques	_____	Principles of internal control
_____	Cash	_____	Purchase order
_____	Cash Over and Short account	_____	Purchase requisition
_____	Cheque	_____	Receiving report
_____	Collusion	_____	Separation of duties
_____	Deposit slip	_____	Signature card
_____	Electronic funds transfer	_____	Vendee
_____	Internal control system	_____	Vendor
_____	Invoice	_____	Voucher
_____	Invoice approval form	_____	Voucher system

1. Lists the items such as currency, coins, and cheques deposited along with each of their dollar amounts.

2. A document containing a checklist of steps necessary for approving an invoice for recording and payment; also called cheque authorization form.

3. A ratio used to assess a company's ability to cover its current debts with existing assets calculated as quick assets (cash, short term investments, and receivable) divided by current liabilities; also called quick ratio.

4. A business paper used by the purchasing department to place an order with the seller (vendor); authorizes the vendor to ship the ordered merchandise at the stated price and terms.

5. Includes the signatures of each person authorized to sign cheques from the account.

6. An internal business paper (or "folder") used to accumulate other papers and information needed to control cash disbursements and to ensure that the transaction is properly recorded.

7. An analysis that explains the difference between the balance of a chequing account shown in the depositor's records and the balance reported on the bank statement.

8. A characteristic of an asset that refers to how easily the asset can be converted into cash or another type of asset or used in paying for services or obligations.

9. An income statement account used to record cash shortages and cash overages arising from omitted petty cash receipts and from errors in making change.

10. Fundamental principles of internal control that apply to all companies requiring management to establish responsibility, maintain adequate records, insure assets and bond key employees, separate recordkeeping from custody of assets, divide responsibility for related transactions, apply technological controls, and perform regular and independent reviews.

11. A business paper listing the merchandise needed by a department and requests that it be purchased.

12. Those current assets which are most liquid, specifically, cash, short-term investments, and receivables.

13. A document signed by the depositor instructing the bank to pay a specified amount of money to a designated recipient.

14. All the policies and procedures managers use to protect assets, ensure reliable accounting, promote efficient operations, and urge adherence to company policies.

15. Cheques that the bank ahs paid and deducted from the customer's account during the month.

16. A set of procedures and approvals designed to control cash disbursements and acceptance of obligations.

17. A form used within a company to notify the appropriate persons that ordered goods are received and to describe the quantities and condition of the goods.

18. An insurance policy purchased by a company to protect against loss from theft by that employee.

19. An itemized statement of goods prepared by the vendor that lists the customer's name, the items sold, the sales prices, and the terms of sale.

20. The use of electronic communication to transfer cash from one party to another.

21. An asset such as cash that is easily converted into other types of assets or used to buy services or to pay liabilities.

22. An act where two or more people agree to commit a fraud.

23. The seller of goods or services, usually a manufacturer or wholesaler.

24. Includes currency, coins, and amounts on deposit in bank chequing or savings accounts.

25. An internal control principle requiring the division of responsibility for related transactions between two or more individuals or departments.

26. The buyer or purchaser of goods or services.

Problem IV

Complete the following by filling in the blanks.

1. If a cashier errs while making change and gives a customer too much money back, the resulting cash shortage is recorded with a debit to an account called _____.

2. A(n) _____ form is used by the accounting department in checking and approving an invoice for recording and payment.

3. Cash discounts offered but not taken are _____.

4. If the size of the petty cash fund remains unchanged, the Petty Cash account _____ (is, is not) debited in the entry to replenish the petty cash fund.

5. Control of a small business is commonly gained through the direct supervision and active participation of the _____ in the affairs and activities of the business. However, as a business grows, it becomes necessary for the manager to delegate responsibilities and rely on _____ rather than personal contact in controlling the affairs and activities of the business.

6. A properly designed internal control system encourages adherence to prescribed managerial policies; and it also (a) _____
_____ ;
(b) _____
_____ ; and (c) _____
_____ .

7. A good system of internal control for cash requires a _____ of duties so that the people responsible for handling cash and for its custody are not the same people who _____ . It also requires that all cash receipts be deposited in the bank _____ and that all payments, except petty cash payments, be made by _____ .

8. A bank reconciliation is prepared to account for the difference between the _____ and the _____ .

9. An accounting system used to control the incurrence and payment of obligations requiring the disbursement of cash is a _____ .

10. A _____ is commonly used by a selling department to notify the purchasing department of items which the selling department wishes the purchasing department to purchase.

11. The business form commonly used by the purchasing department of a large company to order merchandise is called a(n) _____ .

12. Good internal control follows certain broad principles. These principles are:

(a) Establish responsibilities for each task clearly and to _____ .

(b) Maintain adequate records to help protect _____ by ensuring that employees use prescribed procedures.

(c) _____ assets and _____ key employees.

(d) Separate recordkeeping for assets and _____ of assets.

(e) _____ responsibility for related transactions.

(f) Apply _____ controls such as time clocks or cash registers.

(g) Perform regular and independent _____ to ensure internal control procedures are followed.

13. After preparing a bank reconciliation, journal entries _____ (should, should not) be made to record those items listed as outstanding cheques.

14. The acid-test ratio, like the current ratio, divides _____ by _____ to measure a company's ability to cover current liabilities.

Problem V

On November 5 of the current year Cullen Company drew Cheque No. 23 for $50 to establish a petty cash fund.

1. Give the general journal entry to record the establishment of the fund.

DATE	ACCOUNT TITLES AND EXPLANATION	P.R.	DEBIT	CREDIT

After making a payment from petty cash on November 25, the petty cashier noted that there was only $2.50 cash remaining in the fund. The cashier prepared the following list of expenditures from the fund and requested that the fund be replenished.

Nov. 9	Express freight on merchandise purchased....................................	$ 9.75
12	Miscellaneous expense to clean office...	10.00
15	Office supplies...	3.50
18	Delivery of merchandise to customer...	8.00
23	Miscellaneous expense for collect telegram....................................	3.25
25	Express freight on merchandise purchased....................................	13.00

Cheque No. 97 in the amount of $47.50 was drawn to replenish the fund.

2. In the General Journal below give the entry to record the cheque replenishing the petty cash fund.

DATE	ACCOUNT TITLES AND EXPLANATION	P.R.	DEBIT	CREDIT

Problem VI

Information about the following eight items is available to prepare Blanchet Company's December 31 bank reconciliation.

Two cheques (1) No. 453 and (2) No. 457 were outstanding on November 30. Cheque No. 457 was returned with the December bank statement but Cheque No. 453 was not. (3) Cheque No. 478, written on December 26, was not returned with the cancelled cheques; and (4) Cheque No. 480 for $96 was incorrectly entered in the Cash Disbursements Journal and posted as though it were for $69. (5) A deposit placed in the bank's night depository after banking hours on November 30 appeared on the December bank statement, but (6) one placed there after hours on December 31 did not. (7) Enclosed with the December bank statement was a debit memorandum for a bank service charge and (8) a cheque received from a customer and deposited on December 27 but returned by the bank marked "Not Sufficient Funds."

1. If an item in the above list should not appear on the December 31 bank reconciliation, ignore it. However, if an item should appear, enter its number in a set of parentheses to show where it should be added or subtracted in preparing the reconciliation.

BLANCHET COMPANY

Bank Reconciliation

December 31, 2001

Book balance of cash	$X,XXX	Bank statement balance	$X,XXX
Add:		Add:	
( )		( )	
( )		( )	
( )		( )	
Deduct:		Deduct:	
( )		( )	
( )		( )	
( )		( )	
Reconciled balance..................	$X,XXX	Reconciled balance.........................	$X,XXX

2. Certain of the above items require entries on Blanchet Company's books. Place the numbers of these items within the following parentheses:

(   ), (   ), (   ), (   ), (   ), (   )

Problem VII

The bank statement dated September 30, 2001, for the Roratanga Company showed a balance of $2,876.35 which differs from the $1,879.50 book balance of cash on that date. In attempting to reconcile the difference, the accountant noted the following facts:

1. The bank recorded a service fee of $15 that was not recorded on the books of Roratanga Company.

2. A deposit of $500 was made on the last day of the month but was not recorded by the bank.

3. A cheque for $176 had been recorded on the Roratanga Company books as $167. The bank paid the correct amount.

4. A cheque was written during September but has not been processed by the bank. The amount was $422.85.

5. A cheque for $1,000 is still outstanding from August.

6. A cheque for $100 deposited by Roratanga Company was returned marked "Not Sufficient Funds."

7. A credit memorandum stated that the bank collected a note receivable of $200 for Roratanga Company and charged Roratanga a $2 collection fee. Roratanga Company had not previously recorded the collection.

Prepare, in good form, a bank reconciliation which shows the correct cash balance on September 30, 2001.

Fundamental Accounting Principles, 10th Canadian Edition

Solutions for Chapter 9

Problem I

1. T	6. T
2. T	7. F
3. T	8. F
4. T	
5. T	

Problem II

1. C
2. C
3. C
4. B
5. D

Problem III

Acid-test ratio	3	Liquid asset	21
Bank reconciliation	7	Liquidity	8
Bond	18	Quick assets	12
Cancelled cheques	15	Principles of internal control	10
Cash	24	Purchase order	4
Cash Over and Short account	9	Purchase requisition	11
Cheque	13	Receiving report	17
Collusion	22	Separation of duties	25
Deposit slip	1	Signature card	5
Electronic funds transfer	20	Vendee	26
Internal control system	14	Vendor	23
Invoice	19	Voucher	6
Invoice approval form	2	Voucher system	16

Problem IV

1. Cash Over and Short

2. invoice approval

3. discounts lost

4. is not

5. owner-manager, a system of internal control

6. (a) promotes operational efficiencies; (b) protects the business assets from waste, fraud, and theft; and (c) ensures accurate and reliable accounting data

7. separation, keep the cash records, intact each day, cheque

8. book balance of cash, bank statement balance

9. voucher system

10. purchase requisition

11. purchase order

12. (a) one person; (b) assets; (c) insure, bond; (d) custody; (e) divide; (f) technological; (9) reviews

13. should not

14. quick assets, current liabilities

Problem V

1. Nov. 5	Petty Cash	50.00	
	Cash		50.00
	Established a petty cash fund.		
2. Nov. 25	Transportation-In..	22.75	
	Miscellaneous Expenses	13.25	
	Office Supplies	3.50	
	Delivery Expense	8.00	
	Cash		47.50
	Reimbursed the petty cash fund.		

Problem VI

1.

Book balance of cash	$X,XXX	Bank statement balance..................	$X,XXX
Add:		Add:	
( )		(6)	
Deduct:		Deduct:	
(4)		(1)	
(7)		(3)	
(8)		( )	

2.   (4), (7), (8)

Problem VII

RORATANGA COMPANY
Bank Reconciliation
September 30, 2001

Book balance of cash	$1,879.50	Bank statement balance		$2,876.35
Add:		Add:		
Proceeds of note less collection fee	198.00	Deposit on Sept. 30/01		500.00
	$2,077.50			$3,376.35
Deduct:		Deduct:		
NSF cheque...$100.00		Outstanding cheques:		
Service fee........ 15.00		August...............$1,000.00		
Recording error 9.00	124.00	September 422.85		1.422.85
Reconciled balance..............	$1,953.50	Reconciled balance....................		$1,953.50

CHAPTER 10
RECEIVABLES

Learning Objective 1:

Describe accounts receivable and how they occur and are recorded.

Summary

Accounts receivable refer to amounts due from customers for credit sales. The subsidiary ledger lists the amounts owed by individual customers. Credit sales arise from at least two sources: (1) sales on credit and (2) credit card sales. Sales on credit refers to a company granting credit directly to customers. Credit card sales involve use of a third party issuing a credit card.

Learning Objective 2:

Apply the allowance method to account for accounts receivable.

Summary

Under the allowance method, bad debt expense is estimated at the end of the accounting period by recording a debit to Bad Debt Expense and crediting the Allowance for Doubtful Accounts. When accounts are later identified as being uncollectible, they are written off by debiting the Allowance for Doubtful Accounts and crediting Accounts Receivable.

Learning Objective 3:

Estimate uncollectibles using methods based on sales and accounts receivable.

Summary

Uncollectibles are estimated by focusing on either (a) the income statement relation between bad debt expense and credit sales or (b) the balance sheet relation between accounts receivable and the Allowance for Doubtful Accounts. The first approach emphasizes the matching principle for the income statement. The second approach can include either a simple percent relation with accounts receivable or the aging of accounts receivable. It emphasizes realizable value of accounts receivable for the balance sheet.

Learning Objective 4:

Apply the direct write-off method to account for uncollectible accounts receivable.

Summary

The direct write-off method debits Bad Debt Expense and credits Accounts Receivable when accounts are determined to be uncollectible. This method is acceptable only when the amount of bad debt expense is immaterial.

Learning Objective 5:

Describe a note receivable and the computation of its maturity date and interest.

Summary

A note receivable is a written promise to pay a specified amount of money either on demand or at a definite future date. The maturity date of a note is the day the note (principal and interest) must be repaid. Interest rates are typically stated in annual terms. When a note's time to maturity is more or less than one year, the amount of interest on a note is computed by expressing time as a fraction of one year and multiplying the note's principal by this fraction and the annual interest rate.

Learning Objective 6:

Record notes receivable.

Summary

A note is recorded at its principal amount by debiting the Notes Receivable account. The credit amount is to the asset or service provided in return for the note. Interest is earned from holding a note. This interest is recorded for the time period it is held in the accounting period reported on. When a note is honoured, the payee debits the money received and credits both Notes Receivable and interest Revenue. Dishonoured notes are credited to Notes Receivable and Debited to Accounts Receivable.

Learning Objective 7 (Appendix 10A):

Explain how receivables can be converted to cash before maturity.

Summary

There are three usual means to convert receivables to cash before maturity. First, a company can sell accounts receivable to a factor, who charges a factoring fee. Second, a company can borrow money by signing a note payable that is secured by pledging the accounts receivable. Third, notes receivable can be discounted at a bank, with or without recourse. The full-disclosure principle requires companies to disclose the amount of receivables pledged and the contingent liability for notes discounted with recourse.

Learning Objective 8 (Appendix 10B):

Compute accounts receivable turnover and days' sales uncollected and use them to analyze liquidity.

Summary

Accounts receivable turnover and days' sales uncollected are measures of both the quality and liquidity of accounts receivable. The accounts receivable turnover measure indicates how often, on average, receivables are received and collected during the period and is computed as sales divided by average accounts receivable for the period. Days' sales uncollected is calculated as (accounts receivable divided by net sales) x 365 and is used to estimated how much time is likely to pass before cash receipts from net sales are received equal to the current amount of accounts receivable. Both ratios are compared to those for other companies in the same industry, and with prior years' estimates.

I.   **Accounts Receivable**—a receivable refers to an amount due from another party. Examples include accounts receivable, notes receivable, interest receivable, rent receivable, and tax refund receivable.

    A. Recognizing *Accounts Receivable*: amounts due from customers for credit sales; also called *trade receivables*.

       1. Sales on credit: company must maintain a separate account receivable for each customer and account for bad debts from credit sales. At the time of the sale, debit Accounts Receivable for the full amount of the sale.

       2. Credit card sales:

          a. Bank credit card or debit card: retailer receives cash, net of the credit card fee, immediately upon deposit at the bank of the credit card sales receipt—debit Cash for the amount of sale less the credit card company charge, debit Credit Card Expense for this fee.

          b. Non-Bank credit card: retailer mails the credit card sales receipts and awaits payment—debit Accounts Receivable for the full sales amount. When payment is received, debit Cash for amount received, debit Credit Card Expense for the amount of the fee and credit Accounts Receivable for the full amount of the sale.

    B. Valuing Accounts Receivable—Two methods used to account for uncollectible accounts.

    C. Allowance Method—matches the expected loss from uncollectible accounts receivable against the sales they helped produce in that period.

       1. Recording estimated bad debt expense at the end of the accounting period—debit Bad Debt Expense, credit a contra-asset account called the *Allowance for Doubtful Accounts*.

       2. Method satisfies matching principle—expense is charged in period of related sale.

       3. Accounts Receivable are reported at their estimated realizable value (A/Rec less the balance of the allowance account).

       4. To write off an uncollectible—debit Allowance for Doubtful Accounts, credit Accounts Receivable.

       5. Writing off an uncollectible does not change the estimated realizable value of Accounts Receivable.

       6. Recovery of a bad debt—debit Accounts Receivable and credit Allowance for Doubtful Accounts to reinstate the account; then debit Cash and credit Accounts Receivable to record the payment in full.

Chapter Outline

D. Estimating Bad Debt Expense—two methods:

1. *Percent of sales method* (or *income statement method*)—uses income statement relationships. Bad debt expense is calculated as a percentage of credit sales (or net sales).

2. *Accounts Receivable method*s (*balance sheet method*)—uses balance sheet relationships. The required ending credit balance in Allowance for Doubtful Accounts is calculated as:

   a. Percentage of outstanding receivables—adjust Allowance for Doubtful Accounts (debit or credit) to achieve desired ending balance, and (credit or debit) Bad Debt Expense.

   b. Aging accounts receivable—same journal entry accounts.

E. Direct Write Off Method—records the loss from an uncollectible account receivable at the time it is determined to be uncollectible. No attempt is made to estimate uncollectible accounts or bad debt expense.

1. To write off an uncollectible: debit Bad Debt Expense, credit Accounts Receivable.

2. Matching principle—this method does not match revenues and expenses. Bad debt expense is not recorded until an account becomes uncollectible, often not occurring during the same account period.

3. Materiality principle—permits use of this method when bad debt expenses are very small in relation to other financial statement items such as sales and net income.

II. **Notes Receivable**—(*promissory note*) is a written promise to pay a specified amount of money *(principal)* either on demand or at a definite future date. Usually interest-bearing.

A. Promissory notes are notes payable to the *maker* of the note and notes receivable to the *payee* of the note.

B. Maturity date—the date the note is due for payment, calculated as the date of the note plus the time period of the note (days, months or years).

C. Calculating interest

$$\text{Principal of note} \times \text{Annual rate of interest} \times \text{Time expressed in years} = \text{Interest}$$

D. Receipt of a note—debit Notes Receivable for principal or face amount of note. Credit account will depends on reason note is received.

E. End of period interest adjustment—accrued interest is computed and recorded; debit Interest Receivable and credit Interest Revenue.

    F. Honouring the note—when the maker pays the note at maturity, debit Cash for maturity value (face + interest), credit Note Receivable for face amount and credit Interest Revenue (and possibly Interest Receivable) for the interest amount.

    G. Dishonouring the note—when the maker does not pay the note at maturity, debit Accounts Receivable for maturity value (face + interest), credit Note Receivable for face amount and credit Interest Earned for the interest amount.

III.   **Converting Receivables to Cash before Maturity**—reasons for this include the need for cash or a desire to not be involved in collection activities.

    A. Selling Accounts Receivable—buyer, called a *factor*, charges the seller a *factoring fee* and then collects the receivables as they come due.

    B. Pledging Accounts Receivable as Loan Security
        1. Borrower retains ownership of the receivables.
        2. If borrower defaults on the loan, the lender has the right to be paid from receipts as the accounts receivable are collected.
        3. The pledge should be disclosed in notes to financial statement.

    C. Discounting Notes Receivable—selling collection rights to bank or financial institution.
        1. With recourse—if the original maker of note fails to pay the bank when it matures, the original payee must pay.
            a. A company that discounts the note has a *contingent liability* (an obligation to make a future payment if, and only if, an uncertain future event occurs) if maker defaults.
        2. Without recourse—no contingent liability. Bank assumes the risk of a bad debt loss.

    D. Full-Disclosure—of contingent liabilities is required.

IV.   **Using the Information**

    A. *Accounts Receivable Turnover*
        1. Indicates how often receivables are received and collected during the period.
        <u>2.</u> Calculated as: $\dfrac{\text{Net sales}}{\text{Average accounts receivable}}$

    B. *Days' Sales Uncollected*
        1. Estimates how much time is likely to pass before receipt of cash from credit sales is equal to the current amount of accounts receivable.
        <u>2.</u> Calculated as: $\dfrac{\text{Ending inventory}}{\text{Cost of goods sold}} \times 365$

VISUAL # 15
METHODS OF ACCOUNTING FOR BAD DEBTS

	DIRECT WRITE-OFF METHOD	ALLOWANCE METHOD
	Accounts for bad debts from an uncollectible account receivable at the time account is determined to be uncollectible.	At the end of each accounting period, bad debts expense is estimated and recorded.
Year end	No adjusting entry	Adjusting entry required: **Bad Debt Expense XXX** **Allowance for Uncollectible Accounts XXX** (The amount is an estimate based on a percent of sales or a percent of outstanding accounts receivable. If the estimate is based on sales, the full estimate is used in the adjusting entry. If the estimate is based on accounts receivable the allowance account balance is brought to the amount of the estimate.)

When an account is determined to be uncollectible.	Write-off entry required:
	Bad Debts Expense XXX
	  Accounts Receivable/Customer XXX
	(The amount is the balance of the uncollectible account.)
		Write-off entry required:
		Allowance for Uncollectible Accounts XXX
		  Accounts Receivable/Customer XXX
		(The amount is the balance of the uncollectible account.)

When an account previously written off is recovered.	1. Reinstate account *by reversing write-off:*
	Accounts Receivable/Customer XXX
	  Bad Debts Expense XXX
	(The amount is the account balance that was written off.)
	2. Record collection on account normally:
	Cash XXX
	  Accounts Receivable/Customer XXX
	(The amount is the amount collected.)
		1. Reinstate account *by reversing write-off:*
		Accounts Receivable/Customer XXX
		  Allowance for Uncollectible Accounts XXX
		(The amount is the account balance that was written off.)
		2. Record collection on account normally:
		Cash XXX
		  Accounts Receivable/Customer XXX
		(The amount is the amount collected.)

Advantages:	• Does not require adjusting entry. • Does not require year-end estimating of uncollectibles.	• Matches expense against related revenues. • Reports the net realizable accounts receivable on the Balance Sheet (a more accurate reporting of assets).
Disadvantages:	• Violates matching, therefore only allowed if qualified under materiality principle. (May be used by a business that anticipates an immaterial amount of uncollectibles.)	• Requires adjusting entry. • Requires year-end estimating of uncollectibles.

Fundamental Accounting Principles, 10th Canadian Edition

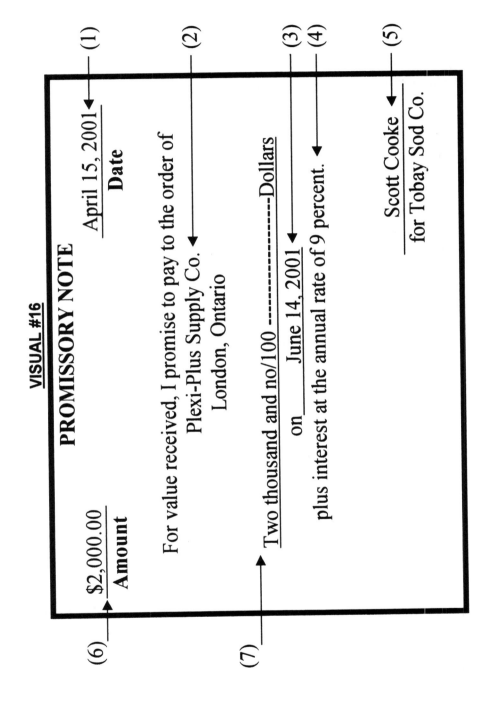

VISUAL #16

PROMISSORY NOTE

April 15, 2001 ←——— (1)
Date

For value received, I promise to pay to the order of
Plexi-Plus Supply Co. ←——— (2)
London, Ontario

Two thousand and no/100 -----------Dollars
on____June 14, 2001————— (3)
————— (4)
plus interest at the annual rate of 9 percent.

Scott Cooke ←——— (5)
for Tobay Sod Co.

$2,000.00
Amount ←——— (6)

(7) ↑

Problem I

The following statements are either true or false. Place a (T) in the parentheses before each true statement and an (F) before each false statement.

1. (   ) Accounts receivable are also known as trade receivables.

2. (   ) If cash from credit card sales is received immediately when the credit card receipts are deposited at the bank, the credit card expense is recorded at the time the sale is recorded.

3. (   ) Businesses with credit customers must maintain a separate account for each customer.

4. (   ) After all entries are posted, the sum of the balances in the Accounts Receivable Ledger should be equal to the balance of the Accounts Receivable account in the General Ledger.

5. (   ) Under the allowance method of accounting for bad debts, accounts receivable are reported on the balance sheet at the amount of cash proceeds expected from their collection.

6. (   ) Under the allowance method of accounting for bad debts, at the time an adjusting entry to record estimated bad debt expense is made, the credit side of the entry is to Accounts Receivable.

7. (   ) Under the allowance method of accounting for bad debts, when an account deemed uncollectible is written off against Allowance for Doubtful Accounts, the estimated realizable amount of Accounts Receivable is decreased.

8. (   ) The journal entry to record recovery of a bad debt returns the amount paid to accounts receivable.

9. (   ) The income statement approach to estimating bad debts is based on the idea that some percentage of credit sales will be uncollectible.

10. (   ) The balance sheet approach to estimating bad debts is based on the idea that some particular percentage of a company's credit sales will become uncollectible.

11. (   ) Aging of accounts receivable requires the examination of each account in the accounts receivable ledger.

12. (   ) The direct write-off method of accounting for bad debts records the loss from an uncollectible account receivable at the time it is determined to be uncollectible.

13. (   ) Although the direct write-off method of accounting for bad debts usually mismatches revenues and expenses, it may be allowed in cases where bad debt losses are immaterial in relation to total net sales and net income.

14. (   ) A promissory note is a unwritten promise the pay a specified amount of money either on demand or at a definite future date.

15. (   ) At maturity, the principle plus the interest owing on a note must be paid.

16. (   ) A 90-day note, dated August 17, matures on November 16.

17. (   ) When notes receivable are outstanding at the end of an accounting period, accrued interest is computed and recorded only at the maturity date.

18. (   ) When a note receivable is discounted without recourse, the bank does not assume the risk of a bad debt loss.

19. (   ) When a note receivable is discounted with recourse, the company that discounts the note has a contingent liability.

20. (   ) A company that pledges its accounts receivable as security for a loan should disclose the fact in a note to the financial statements.

Problem II

You are given several words, phrases, or numbers to choose from in completing each of the following statements or in answering the following questions. In each case select the one that best completes the statement or answers the question and place its letter in the answer space provided.

_____ 1. Pine Company uses the income statement method to calculate its bad debts, and the allowance to account for them. During the year, the credit Sales amounted to $320,000, and at the end of the year, outstanding accounts receivable amounted to $7,500. It was estimated that 4% of sales were uncollectible. What is the year-end adjusting journal entry to record bad debts?

a.	Accounts receivable..	7,500.00	
	Allowance for doubtful accounts		7,500.00
b.	Allowance for doubtful accounts..........................	9,600.00	
	Bad debts expense..		9,600.00
c.	Bad debts expense	300.00	
	Cash..		300.00
d.	Cash..	300.00	
	Bad debts expense..		300.00
e.	Bad debts expense	9,600.00	
	Allowance for doubtful accounts		9,600.00

_____ 2. Granite Company uses the direct write-off method to calculate and account for bad debts. During the year, Sales amounted to $115,000, and at the end of the year, outstanding accounts receivable amounted to $4,500. Crisscross Company's account, for $215, was written off with the journal entry:

a.	Bad debts expense	4,500.00	
	Allowance for doubtful accounts		4,500.00
b.	Bad debts expense	215.00	
	Accounts receivable		215.00
c.	Allowance for doubtful accounts..........................	215.00	
	Accounts receivable		215.00
d.	Accounts for doubtful accounts..........................	4,500.00	
	Bad debts expense..		4,500.00
e.	Accounts receivable..	215.00	
	Bad debts expense..		215.00

_____ 3. Orion Company has decided to write off the account of Jack Irwin against the Allowance for Doubtful Accounts. The $2,100 balance in Irwin's account originated with a credit sale in July of last year. What is the general journal entry to record this write-off?

a.	Allowance for Doubtful Accounts..........................	2,100	
	Accounts Receivable—Jack Irwin		2,100
b.	Accounts Receivable..	2,100	
	Allowance for Doubtful Accounts......................		2,100
c.	Bad debt Expense	2,100	
	Allowance for Doubtful Accounts......................		2,100
d.	Accounts Receivable..	2,100	
	Accounts Receivable—Jack Irwin		2,100
e.	Bad Debt Expense	2,100	
	Accounts Receivable		2,100

_____ 4. Hitech Corporation had credit sales of $3,000,000 in 2001. Before recording the December 31, 2001, adjustments, the company's Allowance for Doubtful Accounts had a credit balance of $1,400. A schedule of the December 31,2001, accounts receivable by age is summarized as follows:

December 31, 2001 Accounts Receivable	Age of Accounts Receivable	Uncollectible Percent Expected
$285,000	Not due	1.5
87,000	1–45 days past due	8.2
34,000	46–90 days past due	37.0
8,000	Over 90 days past due	70.0

Calculate the amount that should appear on the December 31, 2001, balance sheet as allowance for doubtful accounts.

a. $28,189.
b. $5,600.
c. $25,314.
d. $30,989.
e. $29,589.

_____ 5. Based on the information given in problem 4, what is the general journal entry to record bad debt expense for 2001?

a. Debit Bad Debt Expense; credit Allowance for Doubtful Accounts.
b. Debit Accounts Receivable; credit Allowance for Doubtful Accounts.
c. Debit Bad Debt Expense; credit Accounts Receivable.
d. Debit Allowance for Doubtful Accounts; credit Bad Debt Expense.
e. Debit Accounts Receivable; credit Bad Debt Expense.

_____ 6. MBC Company discounts a $25,000 note receivable, with recourse, and receives proceeds of $25,250. MBC's entry to record the transaction would include the following:

a. $25,250 debit to Cash.
b. $250 debit to Interest Expense.
c. $250 debit to Loss on Sale of Notes.
d. $24,750 credit to Notes Receivable.
e. None of the above.

_____ 7. Westing Company had net sales of $500,000 and $400,000 for 2002 and 2001, respectively. Accounts receivable at December 31, 2002 and 2001, were $45,000 and $55,000. What is Westing's accounts receivable turnover for 2002?

a. 11.1 times.
b. 10.0 times.
c. 20.0 times.
d. 9.0 times.
e. None of the above.

_____ 7. Hexagon Company had inventory of $128,000 at the beginning of the year and $152,000 at the end. Cost of goods sold for the year amounted to $1,260,000. What is the company's days' sales in inventory?

   a. 8.3 days.
   b. 37.1 days
   c. 44.0 days
   d. 307.5 days.
   e. None of the above.

Problem III

Many of the important ideas and concepts discussed in Chapter 10 are reflected in the following list of key terms. Test your understanding of these terms by matching the appropriate definitions with the terms. Record the number identifying the most appropriate definition in the blank space next to each term.

_____ Accounts receivable
_____ Accounts receivable method
_____ Accounts receivable turnover
_____ Aging of accounts receivable
_____ Allowance for Doubtful Accounts
_____ Allowance method of accounting
         for bad debts
_____ Bad debts
_____ Balance sheet method
_____ Contingent liability
_____ Days' sales uncollected
_____ Days' sales in receivables
_____ Direct write-off method of
         Accounting for bad debts

_____ Dishonouring a note
_____ Honouring a note receivable
_____ Income statement method
_____ Interest
_____ Maker of a note
_____ Maturity date of a note
_____ Payee of a note
_____ Percent of sales method
_____ Percent of accounts receivable method
_____ Principal of a note
_____ Promissory note
_____ Realizable value
_____ Uncollectible accounts

_____

1. The accounts of customers who do not pay what they have promised to pay; the amount is an expense of selling on credit; also called uncollectible accounts.

2. A method of estimating bad debts which assumes a percent of outstanding receivables in uncollectible.

3. When a note's maker is unable or refuses to pay at maturity.

4. The expected proceeds from converting assets into cash.

5. A contra assets account with a balance equal to the estimated amount of accounts receivable that will be uncollectible; also called the Allowance for Uncollectible Accounts.

6. A measure of both the quality and liquidity of accounts receivable; t indicates how often, on average, receivables are received and collected during the period; computed by dividing credit sales (or net sales) by the average accounts receivable balance.

7. One who signs a note and promises to pay it at maturity.

8. A written promise to pay a specified amount of money either on demand or at a definite future date.

9. An accounting procedure that (1) estimates and reports bad debt expense from credit sales during the period of the sales, and (2) reports accounts receivable as the amount of cash proceeds that is expected from their collection (their estimated realizable value).

10. Uses income statement relations to estimate bad debts; also known as the income statement method.

11. A measure of the liquidity of receivables computed by taking the current balance of receivables and dividing by the credit (or not) sales over the year just completed, and then multiplying by 365 (the number of days in a year); also called day's sales in receivables.

12. Another name for bad debts.

13. Another name for the Percent of sales method.

14. A process of classifying accounts receivable in terms of how long they have been outstanding for the purpose of estimating the amount of uncollectible accounts.

15. Another name for days' sales uncollected.

16. The date on which a note and any interest are due and payable.

17. An obligations to make a future payment if, and only if, an uncertain future event actually occurs.

18. The amount that the signer of a promissory note agrees to pay back when it matures, not including the interest.

19. A method of estimating bad debts using balance sheet relations; also know as balance sheet method.

20. A method of accounting for bad debts that records the loss from an uncollectible account receivable at the time it is determined to be uncollectible; no attempt is made to estimate uncollectible accounts or bad debt expense.

21. The charge for using (not paying) money until a later date.

22. Amounts due from customers for credit sales.

23. When the maker of a note pays the note in full at maturity.

24. The one to whom a promissory note is made payable.

25. Another name for the accounts receivable method.

Problem IV

On December 12, Robind Company received from Jerry Spring, a customer, $300 in cash and a $1,500, 12%, 60-day note dated December 11 in granting a time extension on Hall's past-due account. On December 31, Robind Company recorded the accrued interest on the note, and Jerry Spring paid the note and its interest on the following February 9. Complete the general journal entries to record these transactions.

DATE	ACCOUNT TITLES AND EXPLANATION	P.R.	DEBIT	CREDIT
Dec. 12				
	Received cash and a note in granting a time extension			
	on a past-due account.			
31				
	To record accrued interest on a note receivable.			
Feb. 9				
	Received payment of a note and interest.			

Problem V

On March 1 Robind Company accepted a $1,200, 12%, 60-day note dated that day from a customer, Rosie McNeal, in granting a time extension on the customer's past-due account. When Robind Company presented the note for payment on April 30, it was dishonoured, and on December 20 Robind Company wrote off the debt as uncollectible. Present entries to record the dishonour and the write-off against the company's Allowance for Doubtful Accounts.

DATE	ACCOUNT TITLES AND EXPLANATION	P.R.	DEBIT	CREDIT
Apr. 30				
	To change the account of Rosie McNeal for her			
	dishonoured $1,200, 12%, 60-day note.			
Dec. 20				
	To write off the uncollectible note of Rosie McNeal.			

3333

333333

33333333

Problem VI

On April 2 Robind Company received from Juliet Larkin, a customer, a $1,000, 12%, 60-day note dated that day in granting a time extension on his past-due account. Robind Company held the note until April 26 and then discounted it, with recourse, at its bank. The proceeds from discounting the note were $1,030.00. Complete the following

DATE	ACCOUNT TITLES AND EXPLANATION	P.R.	DEBIT	CREDIT
Apr. 2				
	Received a note in granting a time extension on a			
	past-due account			
26				
	Discounted the Juliet Larkin note.			

Problem VII

Coastal Company uses the allowance method in accounting for bad debt losses, and over the past several years it has experienced an average loss equal to one-fourth of 1% of its credit sales. During 2001 the company sold $928,000 of merchandise on credit, including a $98 credit sale to Gary Bellini on March 5, 2001. The $98 had not been paid by the year's end.

1. If at the end of 2001 Coastal Company, in providing for estimated bad debt losses, assumes history will repeat, it will provide an allowance for 2001 estimated bad debts equal to _____ % of its $928,000 of 2001 charge sales; and the adjusting entry to record the allowance will appear as follows: (Complete the following entry.)

DATE	ACCOUNT TITLES AND EXPLANATION	P.R.	DEBIT	CREDIT
2001				
Dec. 31				
	To record estimated bad debts			

2. The debit of the foregoing entry is to the expense account, _____ _____, which is closed to the _____ account at the end of the accounting period, just as any other expense account is closed.

3. The effect of the foregoing adjusting entry on the 2001 income statement of Coastal Company is to cause an estimated amount of bad debt expense to be deducted from the $928,000 of revenue from 2001 charge sales. This complies with the accounting principle of _____ _____.

4. The credit of the foregoing adjusting entry is to the contra account _____ _____. On the December 31, 2001, balance sheet the balance of this contra account is subtracted from the balance of the _____ account to show the amount that is expected to be realized from the accounts receivable.

5. On March 31, 2002, the Accounts Receivable controlling account and the Allowance for Doubtful Accounts account of Coastal Company had the following balances:

Accounts Receivable		Allowance for Doubtful Accounts	
Mar. 31 65,625			Mar. 31 4,475

A balance sheet which was prepared on March 31, 2002, would show that Coastal Company expects to collect $ _____ of its accounts receivable.

6. On April 1, 2002, Coastal Company decided the $98 account of Gary Bellini (sale made on March 5 of the previous year) was uncollectible and wrote it off as a bad debt. (Complete the entry and post to the above T-accounts the portions affecting the accounts.)

DATE	ACCOUNT TITLES AND EXPLANATION	P.R.	DEBIT	CREDIT
2002				
Apr. 1				
	To write off the account of Gary Bellini			

7. If a balance sheet was prepared immediately after the entry writing off the uncollectible account of Gary Bellini was posted, it would show that Coastal Company expected to collect $ _____ of its accounts receivable. Consequently, the write-off _____ (did, did not) affect the net balance sheet amount of accounts receivable. Likewise, the entry writing off the account did not record an expense because the expense was anticipated and recorded in the _____ _____ entry made on December 31, 2001, the year of the sale.

Problem VIII

Pretzli Company sells almost exclusively for cash, but it does make a few small charge sales, and it also occasionally has a small bad debt loss which it accounts for by the direct write-off method.

1. Give below the entry made by Pretzli Company on February 5 to write off the $55 uncollectible account of Joan Bond (the goods were sold during the previous period.)

DATE	ACCOUNT TITLES AND EXPLANATION	P.R.	DEBIT	CREDIT
Feb. 5				

2. Writing off the foregoing bad debt directly to the Bad Debt Expense account violates the accounting principle of _____.
However, due to the accounting principle _____
the direct write-off is permissible in this case because the company's bad debt losses are very small in relation to its sales.

Problem IX

A company that ages its accounts receivable and increases its allowance for doubtful accounts to an amount sufficient to provide for estimated bad debts had a $75 debit balance in its Allowance for Doubtful Accounts account on December 31. If on that date it estimated that $1,800 of its accounts receivable were uncollectible, it should make a year-end adjusting entry crediting $ _____ to its Allowance for Doubtful Accounts account.

Problem X

Windsor Company allows its customers to use two credit cards: the University National Bank credit card and the Community Credit Card. Using the information given below, prepare general journal entries for Windsor Company to record the following credit card transactions:

a) University National Bank charges a 3% service fee for sales on its credit card. As a commercial customer of the bank, Windsor Company receives immediate credit when it makes its daily deposit of sales receipts.

    May 2   Sold merchandise for $525 to customers who used the University National Bank credit card.

DATE	ACCOUNT TITLES AND EXPLANATION	P.R.	DEBIT	CREDIT

b) Community Credit Card Company charges 4% of sales for use of its card. Windsor Company submits accumulated sales receipts to Community Company and is paid within 30 days.

    May 3   Sold merchandise for $675 to customers using the Community Credit Card. Submitted receipts to Community Company for payment

       30   Received amount due from Community Credit Card Company.

DATE	ACCOUNT TITLES AND EXPLANATION	P.R.	DEBIT	CREDIT

Solutions for Chapter 10

Problem I

1. T	11. T
2. T	12. T
3. T	13. T
4. T	14. F
5. T	15. T
6. F	16. F
7. F	17. F
8. T	18. F
9. T	19. T
10. F	20. T

Problem II

1. E
2. B
3. A
4. E
5. A
6. C
7. B

Problem III

Accounts Receivable	22
Accounts receivable method	19
Accounts receivable turnover	6
Aging of accounts receivable	14
Allowance for Doubtful Accounts	5
Allowance method of accounting for bad debts	9
Bad debts	1
Balance sheet method	25
Contingent liability	17
Days' sales uncollected	11
Days' sales in receivables	15
Direct write-off method of Accounting for bad debts	20
Dishonouring a note	3
Honouring a note	23
Interest	21
Income statement method	13
Maker of a note	7
Maturity date of a note	16
Payee of a note	24
Percent of sales method	10
Percent of accounts receivable method	2
Principal of a note	18
Promissory note	8
Realizable value	4
Uncollectible accounts	12

Problem IV

Dec. 12	Cash	300.00	
	Notes Receivable	1,500.00	
	Accounts Receivable—Jerry Spring		1,800.00
31	Interest Receivable ($1,500 × .12 × 20/365)	9.86	
	Interest Earned		9.86
Feb 9	Cash	1,529.59	
	Interest Receivable		9.86
	Interest Earned ($1,500 × .12 × 40/365)		19.73
	Notes Receivable		1,500.00

Problem V

Apr. 30	Accounts Receivable—Rosie McNeal....................................	1,224.00		
	Interest Earned		23.67	
	Notes Receivable		1,200.00	
Dec. 20	Allowance for Doubtful Accounts......................................	1,223.67		
	Accounts Receivable—Rosie McNeal		1,223.67	

Problem VI

Apr. 2	Notes Receivable...	1,000.00		
	Accounts Receivable—Juliet Larkin.............................		1,000.00	
26	Cash	1,030.00		
	Notes Receivable		1,000.00	
	Interest revenue		30.00	

Problem VII

1. One-fourth of 1%, or .25%

Dec. 31	Bad Debt Expense..	2,320.00		
	Allowance for Doubtful Accounts..............................		2,320.00	

2. Bad Debt Expense, Income Summary
3. Matching revenues and expenses
4. Allowance for Doubtful Accounts, Accounts Receivable
5. $61,150
6.

Apr. 1	Allowance for Doubtful Accounts	98.00	
	Accounts Receivable—Gary Bellini.............................		98.00

Accounts Receivable		Allowance for Doubtful Accounts	
Mar. 31 65,625			Mar. 31 4,475
	Apr. 1 98	Apr. 1 98	

7. $61,150, did not, adjusting.

Problem VIII

1.

Feb. 5	Bad Debt Expense...	55.00	
	Accounts Receivable—Joan Bond		55.00

2. Matching revenues and expenses, materiality

Problem IX

$1,875

Problem X

a) May 2   Cash 509.25
             Credit Card Expense ($525 × 0.03) 15.75
                 Sales 525.00

b) May 3   Accounts Receivable—Community Company 675.00
                 Sales 675.00

       30   Cash 648.00
             Credit Card Expense ($675 × 0.04) 27.00
                 Accounts Receivable—Community Company 675.00

Learning Objective 1:

List the taxes and other items frequently withheld from employees' wages.

Summary

Amounts withheld from employees' wages include federal income taxes, Canada Pension Plan, and employment insurance. Payroll costs levied on employers include employment insurance and Canada Pension. An employee's gross pay may be the employee's specified wage rate multiplied by the total hours worked plus an overtime premium rate multiplied by the number of overtime hours worked. Alternatively, it may be the given periodic salary of the employee. Taxes withheld and other deductions for items such as union dues, insurance premiums, and charitable contributions are subtracted from gross pay to determine the net pay.

Learning Objective 2:

Make the calculations necessary to prepare a Payroll Register, and prepare the entry to record payroll liabilities.

Summary

A Payroll Register is used to summarize all employees' hours worked, regular and overtime pay, payroll deductions, net pay, and distribution of gross pay to expense accounts during each pay period. It provides the necessary information for journal entries to record the accrued payroll and to pay the employees.

Learning Objective 3:

Prepare journal entries to record the payments to employees and explain the operation of a payroll bank account.

Summary

A payroll bank account is a separate account that is used solely for the purpose of paying employees. Each pay period, an amount equal to the total net pay of all employees is transferred from the regular bank account to the payroll bank account. Then cheques are drawn against the payroll bank account for the net pay of the employees.

Learning Objective 4:

Calculate the payroll costs levied on employers and prepare the entries to record the accrual and payment of these amounts.

Summary

When a payroll is accrued at the end of each pay period, payroll deductions and levies also should be accrued with debits and credits to the appropriate expense and liability accounts.

Learning Objective 5:

Calculate and record employee fringe benefit costs and show the effect of these items on the total cost of employing labour.

Summary

Fringe benefit costs that involve simple cash payments by the employer should be accrued with an entry similar to the one used to accrue payroll levies. Legislated employee benefits related to Workers' Compensation and vacation pay are paid for by the employer.

Chapter Outline

I. Payroll Accounting

A. Records cash payments to employees.

B. Provides valuable information regarding labour costs.

C. Accounts for amounts withheld from employees' pay.

D. Accounts for employee (fringe) benefits and payroll costs paid by the employer.

E. Provides the means to comply with governmental regulations on employee compensation.

II. Items Withheld from Employees' Wages

A. Employee's income tax—amount withheld is determined by wages and amount of *personal tax credits*. Deduction tables are provided by *Canada Customs and Revenue Agency (CCRA)*.

B. Canada Pension Plan (CPP)—for working people between ages of 18 and 70. The employer's contribution matches the employee's deduction.

C. Employment Insurance (EI)—for employed people. The employer's contribution equals 1.4 time the employee's deduction. The employer must keep employee records, and, when employment is terminated or interrupted, complete a "Record of Employment".

D. T-4 forms—a year-end statement completed by the employer showing wages and deductions for the year.

E. Union Dues.

F. Other deductions (such as insurance premiums).

III. The Payroll Register

A. Timekeeping—compiling a record of time worked by each employee.

B. Payroll register—summarizes the total hours worked as compiled on clock cards or by other means, for each pay period.

C. Payroll is recorded each pay period with a general journal entry: debits to expense accounts and credits to various payable accounts.

D. Paying the employees

1. Made from a regular chequing account, or

2. Made through a separate payroll bank account.

E. Employee's Individual Earnings Record—provides for each employee, in one record, a full year's summary of the employee's working time, gross earnings, deductions, and net pay. The information is taken from the Payroll Register.

IV.   **Payroll Deductions Required of the Employer**

    A. Canada Pension Plan

    B. Employment Insurance

V.   **Employee (Fringe) Benefit Costs**

    A. Workers' Compensation—paid by the employer

    B. Insurance and retirement plans.

    C. Vacation Pay

Problem I

The following statements are either true or false. Place a (T) in the parentheses before each true statement and an (F) before each false statement.

1. ( ) According to law, a T-4 form showing wages earned and taxes withheld must be given to each employee within one month after the year-end.

2. ( ) Employment insurance is withheld from employees' wages at the rate of 2.4% (2000).

3. ( ) Canada Pension Plan amounts are levied equally on the employee and the employer.

4. ( ) Employee (fringe) benefit costs represent expenses to the employer in addition to the direct costs of salaries and wages.

5. ( ) Each time a payroll is recorded, a general journal entry should also be made to record the employer's employment insurance cost.

6. ( ) Since income taxes withheld from an employee's wages are expenses of the employee, not the employer, they should not be treated as liabilities of the employer.

7. ( ) Since Jacques Company has very few employee accidents, the company has received a very favourable Workers' Compensation rating. As a result, Jacques Company should expect to pay smaller amounts of Worker's Compensation premium than normal.

Problem II

You are given several words, phrases or numbers to choose from in completing each of the following statements or in answering the following questions. In each case select the one that best completes the statement or answers the question and place its letter in the answer space provided

Use the following information as to earning and deductions for the pay period ended November 15 taken from a company's payroll records for the next two questions:

Employee's Name	Earnings to End of Previous Week	Gross Pay This Week	Income Tax	Medical Insurance Deducted
Rita Hawn	$25,700	$ 800	$155.00	$ 35.50
Dolores Hopkins	20,930	800	134.00	35.50
Robert Allen	49,900	1,000	193.00	42.00
Calvin Ingram	18,400	740	128.00	42.00
		$3,340	$610.00	$155.00

_____ 1. Employees' EI and CPP are withheld at an assumed 6% rate on the first $30,000 paid each employee. A general journal entry to accrue the payroll under the assumption that all of the employees work in the office should include a:

   a. Debit to Accrued Payroll Payable for $3,340.
   b. Debit to EI and CPP Payable for $200.40.
   c. Debit to Payroll Expense for $140.40.
   d. Credit to Payroll Expense for $140.40.
   e. Credit to Accrued Payroll Payable for $2,374.60.

_____ 2. Assume that Canada Pension Plan applies at a rate of 3.9% on the $33,400 of eligible earnings. The general journal entry to record the employer's payroll cost resulting from the payroll should include a debit to Salaries Expense for:

   a. $53.44
   b. $127.66
   c. $130.26
   d. $149.76
   e. The entry does not include a debit to Payroll Expense.

_____ 3. In addition to determining and withholding income tax from each employee's wages, employers are required to:

    a. periodically deposit the withheld taxes with Canada Customs and Revenue Agency.

    b. file a quarterly report showing the income taxes withheld.

    c. give each employee a Wage and Tax Statement for the year, Form T-4.

    d. send Canada Customs and Revenue Agency copies of all T-4 forms given employees.

    e. All of the above.

Problem III

Many of the important ideas and concepts that are discussed in Chapter 11 are reflected in the following list of key terms. Test your understanding of these terms by matching the appropriate definitions with the terms. Record the number identifying the most appropriate definition in the blank space next to each term.

_____ Canada Pension Plan   _____ Employee's net pay

_____ Clock card   _____ Payroll bank account

_____ Employee fringe benefits   _____ Payroll deduction

_____ Employment insurance   _____ Personal tax credit

_____ Employee's gross pay   _____ Timekeeping

_____ Employee's Individual Earnings Record   Wage bracket withholding table

1. An amount deducted from an employee's pay, usually based on the amount of an employee's gross pay.

2. An employment/employer-financed unemployment insurance plan.

3. A special bank account a company uses solely for the purpose of paying employees by depositing in the account each pay period an amount equal to the total employees' net pay and drawing the employees' payroll cheques on the account.

4. The amount an employee is paid, determined by subtracting from gross pay all deductions for taxes and other items that are withheld from the employee's earnings.

5. A national contributory retirement pension scheme.

6. A table showing the amounts to be withheld from employees' wages at various levels of earnings.

7. Payments by an employer, in addition to wages and salaries, that are made to acquire employee benefits such as insurance coverage and retirement income.

8. A record of an employee's hours worked, gross pay, deductions, net pay, and certain personal information about the employee.

9. Amounts that may be deducted from an individual's income taxes and that determine the amount of income taxes to be withheld.

10. A card issued to each employee that the employee inserts in a time clock to record the time of arrival and departure to and from work.

11. The process of recording the time worked by each employee.

12. The amount an employee earns before any deductions for taxes or other items such as union dues or insurance premiums.

Problem IV

Complete the following by filling in the blanks.

1. An employee who works 45 hours in one week must normally be paid his or her regular rate of pay for the 45 hours plus overtime premium pay at one-half his or her regular rate for _____ of the 45 hours.

2. Funds for the payment of federal retirement benefits are raised by payroll deductions imposed under a law called the _____
   _____.

3. The amount to be withheld from an employee's wages for federal income taxes is determined by
   (a)_____
   and (b)_____.

4. Weekly employment benefits received by workers are based on _____
   _____prior to employment ceasing.

5. The Canada Pension Plan Act levies a payroll tax on both covered employers and their employees. In 2000, an employer was required to withhold CPP deductions from the wages of employees at the rate of _____% of each employee's gross earnings in excess of the allowed exemption, the withholding to continue each year until the contribution exempt point is reached. In addition to the employee's CPP withholdings, an employer must also pay a CPP amount equal to the sum of the _____ withheld from the wages of all of its employees.

6. The computation of income tax withholding deductions is facilitated by the use of _____
   _____ provided by Canada Customs and Revenue Agency.

7. Employers are required to remit the payroll deductions and withheld income taxes to the _____
   _____ on or before the _____
   _____ following that in which withholdings were made.

8. On or before the last day of _____following each year, an employer must give each employee a _____. A summary of information contained in the _____ supported by copies of statements issued to the employees is forwarded to the _____
   _____.

9. Worker's compensation premiums are paid in total by the _____
   _____and are normally
   based on (a) _____and
   (b) _____.

Problem V

The Payroll Register of Newman Sales for the second week of the year follows. It has the deductions and net pay of the first three employees calculated and entered.

1. Mr. Yancy's deductions are as follows:

Canada Pension Plan	$35.33
Employment Insurance	29.81
Income Taxes	220.80
Medical Insurance	25.00

EMPLOYEE'S NAME	CLOCK CARD NUMBER	DAILY TIME M	T	W	T	F	S	S	TOTAL HOURS	O.T. HOURS	REG. PAY RATE		REGULAR PAY	O.T. PREMIUM PAY	GROSS PAY	
Ryan Black	11	8	8	8	7	4	0	0	35		18	00	630 00		630 00	1
Jan Duncan	8	8	8	8	5	4	0	0	33		20	00	660 00		660 00	2
Walter Prince	14	8	8	7	8	4	0	0	35		22	00	770 00		770 00	3
Jack Yancy	5	8	8	8	8	8	4	0	44	4	24	00				4
																5

Week ending January 14, 2001

	DEDUCTIONS EI	CPP	INCOME TAXES	MEDICAL INSURANCE	TOTAL DEDUC-TIONS	PAYMENT NET PAY	CHEQUE NUMBER	DISTRIBUTION SALES SALARIES	OFFICE SALARIES	SHOP SALARIES
1	17 01	20 16	126 00	30 00	193 17	436 83		630 00		
2	17 82	21 12	132 00	28 00	198 94	461 06				660 00
3	20 79	24 64	154 00	25 00	224 43	545 57				770 00
4										
5										

2. Complete the Payroll Register by totalling its columns, and give the general journal entry to record its information.

DATE	ACCOUNT TITLES AND EXPLANATION	P.R.	DEBIT	CREDIT

Newman Sales uses a special payroll bank account in paying its employees. Each payday, after the general journal entry recording the information of its Payroll Register is posted, a single cheque for the total of the employees' net pay is drawn and deposited in the payroll bank account. This transfers funds equal to the payroll total from the regular bank account to the payroll bank account. Then special payroll cheques are written on the payroll bank account and given to the employees. For the January 14 payroll, Cheque No. 845 was used to transfer funds equal to the total of the employees' net pay from the regular bank account. After this, four payroll cheques beginning with payroll Cheque No.102 were drawn and delivered to the employees.

3. Make the entry to record Cheque No. 845 in the Cheque Register below.

4. Enter the payroll cheque numbers in the Payroll Register.

CHEQUE REGISTER

DATE	CH. NO	PAYEE	ACCOUNT DEBITED	P.R.	ACCRUED PAYROLL PAYABLE DR.	CASH CR

5. In the space below give the general journal entry to record the payroll taxes levied on Newman Sales as a result of the payroll entered in its January 14 Payroll Register.

DATE	ACCOUNT TITLES AND EXPLANATION	P.R.	DEBIT	CREDIT

6. On the next page is the individual earnings record of Jack Yancy. Transfer from the Payroll Register to Mr. Yancy's earnings record the payroll data for the second pay period of the year.

EMPLOYEE'S INDIVIDUAL EARNINGS RECORD

EMPLOYEE'S NAME _____ Jack Yancy _____   EMPLOYEE NO. ___5___

HOME ADDRESS _____ 2590 Columbia _____ Street   PHONE NUMBER _____ 965-5698 _____

S.I. ACCT. NO. _____ 119-051- 879 _____

NOTIFY IN CASE OF EMERGENCY _____ Mary Yancy _____

DATE OF TERMINATION _____ REASON _____

EMPLOYED _____ 1/9/83 _____

DATE OF BIRTH _____ May 20, 1948 _____   DATE BECOMES 65 May 20, 2013

MALE (X)   FEMALE ( )   MARRIED (X)   SINGLE ( )

OCCUPATION _____ Manager _____   NUMBER OF DEPENDENTS ___4___   PLACE _____ Store and office _____

PAY RATE _____ $24.00 _____

DATE		TIME LOST		TIME WK.		REG. PAY	O.T. PREM. PAY	GROSS PAY	CPP	EI	INCOME TAXES	MEDICAL INSUR- ANCE	TOTAL DEDUC- TIONS	NET PAY	CHEQUE NUMBER	CUMU- LATIVE PAY
PER. ENDS	PAID	HRS.	REASON	TOTAL	O.T. HOURS											
Jan. 7	Jan. 10	8	NY	32	0	768 00		768 00	24 58	20 74	153 60	25 00	223 92	544 08	095	768 00

Solutions for Chapter 11

Problem I

1.	F	5.	T
2.	T	6.	F
3.	T	7.	T
4.	T		

Problem II

1. E
2. B
3. E

Problem III

Clock Card 7
CPP 5
Employee's gross pay................................2
Employee's individual earnings record..........8
Employee's net pay 1
Employment insurance 10
Gross Pay 2

Income tax withholdings............................6
Payroll bank account..................................9
Payroll tax 11
Receiver General.......................................3
Timekeeping 4
Wage bracket withholding table.................12

Problem IV

1. five

2. Canada Pension Plan

3. (a) the amount of his or her wages,

   (b) the number of his or her exemptions.

4. the average weekly wages.

5. 3.9%; amounts

6. tax withholding tables

7. Receiver General for Canada; 15th of the month

8. February; T-4 statement; T-4 statements; District Taxation Office.

9. employer (a) accident experience of the industrial classification of the business;

   (b) the total payroll.

Problem V

1., 2., 4., & 5.

PAYROLL REGISTER

EMPLOYEE'S NAME	CLOCK CARD NUMBER	M	T	W	T	F	S	S	TOTAL HOURS	O.T. HOURS	REG. PAY RATE		REGULAR PAY		O.T. PREMIUM PAY		GROSS PAY		
Ryan Black	11	8	8	8	7	4	0	0	35		18	00	630	00	0	00	630	00	1
Jan Duncan	8	8	8	8	5	4	0	0	33		20	00	660	00	0	00	660	00	2
Walter Prince	14	8	8	7	8	4	0	0	35		22	00	770	00	0	00	770	00	3
Jack Yancy	5	8	8	8	8	8	4	0	44	4	24	00	1056	00	48	00	1104	00	4
													3116	00	48	00	3164	00	5

Week ending January 14, 2001

	EI		CPP		INCOME TAX		MEDICAL INSURANCE		TOTAL DEDUC-TIONS		NET PAY		CHEQUE NUMBER	SALES SALARIES		OFFICE SALARIES		SHOP SALARIES	
1	17	01	20	16	126	00	30	00	193	17	436	83	102	630	00				
2	17	82	21	12	132	00	28	00	198	94	461	06	103					660	00
3	20	79	24	64	154	00	25	00	224	43	545	57	104					770	00
4	29	81	35	33	220	80	25	00	310	94	793	06	105			1104	00		
5	85	43	101	25	632	80	108	00	927	48	2236	52		630	00	1104	00	1430	00

1. Jan. 7 Sales Salaries Expense 630.00
    Office Salaries Expense 1,104.00
    Shop Salaries Expense 1,430.00
        Canada Pension Plan Payable 101.25
        Employment Insurance Payable 85.43
        Employees' Income Taxes Payable 632.80
        Medical Insurance Payable 108.00
        Accrued Payroll Payable 2,236.52

3.

CHEQUE REGISTER

DATE	CH. NO	PAYEE	ACCOUNT DEBITED	P.R.	ACCRUED PAYROLL PAYABLE DR.		CASH CR	
Jan. 9	845	Payroll Bank						
		Account			2236	52	2236	52

5. Jan. 7 Payroll Taxes Expense 220.85
        Canada Pension Plan Payable 101.25
        Employment Insurance Payable 119.60

EMPLOYEE'S INDIVIDUAL EARNINGS RECORD

EMPLOYEE'S NAME ___Jack Yancy___ S.I. ACCT. NO. ___119-051-879___ EMPLOYEE NO. ___5___

HOME ADDRESS ___2590 Columbia___ Street NOTIFY IN CASE OF EMERGENCY ___Mary Yancy___ PHONE NUMBER ___965-5698___

EMPLOYED ___1/9/83___ DATE OF TERMINATION _____ REASON _____

DATE OF BIRTH ___May 20, 1948___ DATE BECOMES 65 ___May 20, 2013___ MALE (X) FEMALE ( ) MARRIED (X) SINGLE ( ) NUMBER OF DEPENDENTS ___4___ PAY RATE ___$24.00___

OCCUPATION ___Manager___ PLACE ___Store and office___

DATE PER. ENDS	DATE PAID	TIME LOST HRS.	TIME LOST REASON	TIME WK. TOTAL	TIME WK. O.T. HOURS	REG. PAY	O.T. PREM. PAY	GROSS PAY	CPP	EI	INCOME TAXES	MEDICAL INSUR-ANCE	TOTAL DEDUC-TIONS	NET PAY	CHEQUE NUMBER	CUMU-LATIVE PAY
Jan. 7	Jan. 10	8	NY	32	0	768 00		768 00	24 58	20 74	153 60	25 00	223 92	544 08	095	768 00
14	16			44	4	1056 00	48 00	1104 00	35 33	29 81	220 80	25 00	310 94	793 06	105	1872 00